Praise for *Feels Like Home* and Marian Parsons

"Marian Parsons, aka Miss Mustard Seed, is that best friend with great taste every homeowner wishes for. Is there nothing this woman can't do? She paints both furniture and walls; upholsters; sews curtains, bed linens, slipcovers, and even dog beds; and is unafraid to tackle carpentry, tiling, and furniture stripping. In over a decade's worth of blog entries, she's provided her fans—including me—with common sense, attainable tips for DIY home design. Lately, we've watched as she and her husband transformed a blah, builder-beige, thirteen-year-old tract house into a gracious, warm, and inviting sanctuary for their young sons, a big dog, and two mischievous cats. Now, with *Feels Like Home*, Marian has gifted us the ultimate design handbook with sound advice, simplified tutorials, and yes, her trademark gorgeous photography. *Feels Like Home* is the last decorating book this decorator-in-denial will ever need."

—MARY KAY ANDREWS, *NEW YORK TIMES* BESTSELLING AUTHOR OF *THE FIXER UPPER*; *HISSY FIT*; *HELLO, SUMMER*; AND *THE NEWCOMER*

"*Feels Like Home* is an authentic story of how, regardless of your circumstances or your location, the very essence of home is in your heart and in the love that you share there.

"For creatives, often part of the dream for a home is to have a special separate place in which to lose oneself, and to make the impossible possible. But as Marian says, it is not what your home gives to you, but what you create with it and in it that is the foundation upon which your life is built. The reality is that most creatives aspire for their own sanctuary, but even if that dream is indeed their reality, you will often find them at the kitchen table, the heart of any home, creating and sharing what they love with those they love most.

"Like Marian herself, her book is beautiful, hopeful, personal, and inspiring. This is a resource, a handbook, and an inspirational guide to help you create exactly what feels like home for you and those that will share it with you."

—JO PACKHAM, CREATOR AND EDITOR IN CHIEF OF WOMEN CREATE MAGAZINES

"Do you dream of living in a completely custom home made just for you? Does that seem impossible? Well, Marian, aka Miss Mustard Seed, has proven in *Feels Like Home* that designing your dream home isn't a far-fetched idea and is in fact obtainable for everyone who follows her helpful tips in this guidebook filled with all her secrets. You will want to keep this book handy as you are on the journey to make you house your home!"

—LIZ MARIE GALVAN, AUTHOR OF *COZY WHITE COTTAGE* AND BLOGGER AT LIZMARIEBLOG.COM

"Marian speaks to my home-loving heart. Creating an environment, you love to live in is an adventure! We all start from a unique place, right where we are. The path will have some twists and turns, but the home you create will nurture your heart and soul in a way no other journey can. This book will become a well-loved staple in your library, inspiring you with ideas to make any house feel like home."

—MELISSA MICHAELS, *NEW YORK TIMES* BESTSELLING AUTHOR OF *LOVE THE HOME YOU HAVE*, *THE INSPIRED ROOM*, AND *DWELLING*

"Whether it's her interiors or her art, Marian's work epitomizes timeless style rooted in authenticity, great taste, and casual elegance. Everything is inviting and comfy, while elevated and approachable at the same time."

—BRIAN PATRICK FLYNN, INTERIOR DESIGNER HGTV DREAM HOME

"*Feels Like Home* offers the encouragement and guidance needed to help you create a home that reflects your unique style and gives you a sense of belonging when you walk through the doors."

—HEATHER BULLARD, EDITORIAL PROP STYLIST

"*Feels Like Home* is full of ideas, inspiration, and encouragement for finding your style and learning how to decorate your space and make it your own. Marian shares her years of expertise, tips, and advice, along with DIY projects, and shows how to take any style of house and create a welcoming, beautiful home that is perfect for you."

—COURTNEY ALLISON, AUTHOR OF *FRENCH COUNTRY COTTAGE* AND FRENCHCOUNTRYCOTTAGE.NET

"Marian Parson's book *Feels Like Home* is such an inspiring and reassuring resource that brings some very fresh and personal methods toward helping you appreciate and listen to your home, whilst, at the same time exploring the idea of adding to it. There are some great tips, especially about layers and colors, and I love Marian's focus on experimentation and how 'home' will always be a process, not a destination. This is a book which doesn't rely on motivating bold moves—which you may later regret—but instead gently encourages you to work with what you already have, what you already feel, and shows how you can build and grow a real home from those genuine foundations."

—PHILIPPA STANTON, @5FTINF

FEELS LIKE *home*

FEELS LIKE *home*

TRANSFORMING YOUR SPACE
FROM UNINSPIRING TO UNIQUELY YOURS

MARIAN PARSONS

NEW YORK NASHVILLE

Published in association with Jenni Burke of Illuminate Literary Agency, www.illuminateliterary.com

Worthy
Hachette Book Group
1290 Avenue of the Americas, New York, NY 10104
worthypublishing.com
twitter.com/worthypub

First Edition: September 2021

Worthy is a division of Hachette Book Group, Inc. The Worthy name and logo are trademarks of Hachette Book Group, Inc.

The publisher is not responsible for websites (or their content) that are not owned by the publisher.

The Hachette Speakers Bureau provides a wide range of authors for speaking events. To find out more, go to www.hachettespeakersbureau.com or call (866) 376-6591.

Additional photo credits information is on page 289.

Print book interior design by Rita Sowins / Sowins Design.

Library of Congress Cataloging-in-Publication Data has been applied for.

ISBNs: 978-1-5460-1583-3 (hardcover), 978-1-5460-1580-2 (ebook)

Printed in China

APS

10 9 8 7 6 5 4 3 2 1

PREVIOUS PAGE: This may look like the parlor in a historic home, but it's the living room in a 1970s suburban home. Britt and Kelly Noser have thoughtfully decorated the home in antiques found at auctions and consignment shops over the years, creating a space that fits their aesthetic.

to my **Mom,**

From rearranging my room to acting in plays to starting a business,
you have always supported my creative endeavors.
You aren't just a cheerleader on the sidelines, but you put on your
painting clothes and get right in there with me.

Together we've refinished furniture, sewn pillows and curtains,
painted walls, hung wallpaper, installed trim, and countless other projects
through the years. You've edited thousands of blog posts,
freelance articles, and did the initial proof on all of my books.
And you do it all without asking for anything in return.

I am so blessed to have you as my mom. I love you.

contents

Introduction: The Bespoke Home *11*

How to Use This Book *13*

CHAPTER I: WHAT DOES HOME FEEL LIKE? *17*

CHAPTER II: TELLING YOUR STORY BY ADDING CHARACTER *35*

CHAPTER III: LIVING SPACES *61*

CHAPTER IV: KITCHENS *83*

CHAPTER V: DINING SPACES *109*

CHAPTER VI: BEDROOMS *135*

CHAPTER VII: CREATIVE & WORK SPACES *165*

CHAPTER VIII: THE REST OF THE ROOMS *193*

                  (BATHROOMS, HALLS, LAUNDRY ROOMS,

                  FOYERS & MUDROOMS)

CHAPTER IX: CUSTOM FURNISHINGS *213*

CHAPTER X: FINISHING TOUCHES *247*

CHAPTER XI: THE ART OF LOVING YOUR HOME FOR WHAT IT IS *271*

The Befores *284*

Credits *289*

Acknowledgments *290*

Sources *293*

Index *295*

About the Author *303*

Thomas Jefferson's home, Monticello, in the fall of 2013.

INTRODUCTION

the bespoke home

be·spoke	**home**
/bəˈspōk/	/hōm/
adjective	*noun*
made to order	the place where one lives

Imagine walking into a home that was designed, built, and decorated just for you. As you look around the house, every detail feels homey and personal—it reflects your particular style. From the architectural statements in the entryway to the finishing touches in the master suite, the wants and needs of you and your family are brought to life here. This home fits you like a well-tailored suit, and yet is as comfy as your favorite pair of pajamas. As you exhale deeply and settle onto the sofa, you realize this is your dream home. *This feels like home.*

What would that home look like? How would it feel to live in this perfectly customized home?

Okay, let's set this imaginary dream home aside for a moment, because the truth is that most of us will never have a home that fulfills 100 percent of our wildest wishes and desires. Even custom homes are usually based on floor plans that weren't designed specifically for you, but for someone *like you*. And even homes that are designed from scratch for an individual usually end up having one thing or another that doesn't look or function in actuality as it promised to on paper.

Thomas Jefferson, who famously designed his own dream home, Monticello, made many major and minor modifications to it over a period of forty years. Forty years!

So then, is the perfect, customized, bespoke home an elusive dream?

I propose that a bespoke home, a house that feels more like home than any other place in the world, is a process, not a destination. It's not all about aesthetics and architecture, but about the feeling the space evokes.

If owning and living in a bespoke, personalized home is a process, then that offers hope for all of the cookie-cutter, builder-grade, non-custom homes, condos, studios, apartments, and town houses that populate neighborhoods across the US and for the people like us who live in them! We *can* customize each space, one little step at a time, bringing our idea of what feels like home to life, until we delight in each room of our house. It's not perfect, but rather *perfectly suited* to us.

Because you are reading this book, you probably have a general idea of what you like in a home. You may, however, be lacking the confidence, complete vision, or the know-how to execute those ideas in your house. And I know from personal experience and from helping my readers online for over ten years that the idea of tackling one room, much less an entire house, can seem daunting when the finish line is vague. That's why I wrote this book for you. We all might have different starting lines, but we can all *start*! That's truly the first step.

Feels Like Home is the firing shot you need to get started, and it's the coach to guide you along your way. This journey is unique in that there is no time limit, there is no competition, and you are the one who decides where the finish line is. You are the one who determines what home feels like for you and your family. This is not dictated by trends, standards set by designers, or by glossy pictures in magazines or on blogs, Instagram, or Pinterest, but by *you*. The pressure is off when your room doesn't have to be compared to or compete with those standards.

I once stumbled upon a board on Pinterest titled "The Home I'll Never Have." I remember feeling sad for the creator of the board, who filled

it with beautiful images of rooms that felt way out of her reach.

Maybe you feel like that woman. Maybe you *are* that woman and that was your board! Either way, I'm glad you have this book in your hands. As a longtime lover of all things home, with a passion for empowering and inspiring others, I'm excited about encouraging and supporting you. I firmly believe in your ability to transform your home from uninspired to uniquely yours. There is potential under your roof that you may not have thought possible, and together we will find a way to reveal it. You can inspire your home with your character, personality, and charm. I'm going to teach you what I have learned over the years and share how I've transformed my 2004 builder-beige suburban house into a home that feels like ours. Are you ready to join me?

I extend my hand to you as we embrace this journey together.

HOW TO USE THIS BOOK

Well, first of all, you can use this book however you want! (And you are welcome that I am not bossing you around with your own purchase.) But I'd like to give some suggestions, particularly for those who get easily overwhelmed or experience decision fatigue after deciding simply what to eat for breakfast. I don't want this book to feel like a new to-do list. This book isn't asking anything of you or telling you what's beautiful or what's ugly, what's right or what's wrong. This book, first and foremost, should be a resource that inspires and encourages you.

Here are some suggestions to get the most out of this book depending on your area of interest.

Instruction

I have included nine project tutorials in this book and dozens of tips, tools, and suggestions to teach you what I've learned over twenty years of home and decorating projects. If you read decorating books and wish they shared *how* they painted those cabinets or installed that trim, well, you've come to the right book. I'll show you how.

Inspiration

I love to read decorating books, and by "read," I mean flip through them and look at the pictures, seeing what jumps out at me and what I can use in my own spaces. This book can be that, too. Just a place to visit as a jumping-off point for your own creativity. We may have differing design aesthetics, but the principles, ideas, and projects can all be translated to fit your own personal style.

Motivation

This is a key component to transforming a home. Whether you're doing DIY projects, hiring out, or a combination of the two, I hope this book will be like an energy drink that jolts you into action (except longer lasting and more enjoyable). I've included a variety of prompts, exercises, and quick activities that can get you excited and moving! Really, if you're feeling in a funk, just try one of the assignments, and I can almost guarantee you'll be flush with new ideas.

Encouragement

When we take in dozens (if not hundreds) of images scrolling through Instagram or Pinterest, we often miss—or risk missing—this crucial component. We're just seeing beautiful, finished, styled, and photoshopped spaces, and we don't always stop to read the captions. We're missing out on the commentary and the story behind the space…the hard work it took to get there, the tears shed over ordering a mirror that didn't fit, or the can of paint that was accidentally spilled all over the floor mid-project. When we miss the stories and experiences, those beautiful images can feel hollow and even discouraging. It can bring out "must be nice" sorts of feelings. I hope this book will help you slow down, appreciate the patient process, and internalize the idea that you, too, can do this.

FEELS LIKE *home*

CHAPTER I

WHAT DOES *home* FEEL LIKE?

WE SHAPE OUR BUILDINGS AND AFTERWARDS OUR BUILDINGS SHAPE US.
—*WINSTON CHURCHILL*

Whenever I'm asked where I'm from, the answer is complicated. I'm not really from any one particular place.

I grew up in a military family, as an Army brat. BRAT, for those who don't know, means "born, raised, and trapped." It also means we moved a lot, so home was literally a moving target for me. Because the location changed every two to four years until I was an adult, home was never a specific place. Home was people and the things that were packed in the truck and moved with us. It was the homes of my grandparents, which were constant through the years and we would visit during the summers. It was the European style that I fell in love with while growing up on military bases in Germany. It was lush green hills. It was the afghan my great-grandmother crocheted that was always folded over the back of the sofa. It was painted dollhouse furniture. It was smells and sounds and foods and feelings.

For me, home is a result of those good memories mingled with an ideal of new memories I want to create.

As I look at how my home is decorated now as well as how my style has developed over the years, I see that all of my choices lead back to what feels like home to me. While I have consciously made choices based on aesthetics and function, there has always been an underlying current, barely perceptible yet ever present, that, until recently, I didn't even notice. It's the silent question that I never have to consciously ask before I make a purchase:

Does this feel like home?

Expectation, Meet *Reality*

Before we dive deeper into what feels like home, I need to set the stage for you to give you some context for why I wanted to write this book.

When our house hunt in Rochester, Minnesota, began, I made a list of things I wanted in a house and things that, if they were present within those walls, would be deal-breakers for me. I'm sure you've been there before! That list, when stacked against prospective homes on the market, can often require moderate if not drastic compromises.

Some things on my particular wish list were a good floor plan, a gas range, living spaces that were optimized for entertaining, lots of natural light, and extra rooms (or an outbuilding) that could accommodate my home-based business. For our family of four, my husband, Jeff, and I also wanted four bedrooms, a two-car garage (it is Minnesota, after all), and close proximity to the boys' school and my husband's place of work.

This list was based on experience, practicality, and preferences, but it was also based on our idea of home. Any home Jeff and I ever took note of as we drove by fit this idea. We would say things like, "Man, it would feel so good to drive up the driveway to that house every day." That is the kind of house we wanted.

To me, that meant an old house—one with creaky floors and wavy-glassed windows and rich with the stories of families who had lived there through the generations. This was a nonnegotiable for me. I set the search parameters at a maximum date of 1940 and a minimum date of 0. If it was required for us to add electricity,

plumbing, running water, and Wi-Fi, I could live with that. Not really, but it *had to be old*. I felt like my heart needed an old house in order to feel completely and utterly at home there.

At the top of my deal-breaker list was a cookie-cutter suburban home. *Especially* one with a two-story foyer that I considered to be a colossal waste of space that also posed head-scratching decorating challenges. I didn't want a home that was basic, boring, beige, or common. I made the assumption there would always be a disconnect between that kind of house and my idea of home.

At the top of Jeff's deal-breaker list was a fixer-upper. Jeff was a grad student at the time and would be working a new full-time job, and the idea of a full renovation with everything else on his plate was just more than he could stomach.

I started my online search with optimism. I thought of all of the picturesque Minnesota farmhouses dotting the expansive farmlands surrounding Rochester. I dreamed of a hundred-year-old home with good bones and all of the modern amenities. As I dug deeper and deeper in the online listings, I realized that my wish list was all but worthless.

Expectation, meet Reality. You two might not get along.

I am sure I'm not the only one who has approached a house hunt with the giddiness of a girl expecting a pony for her birthday, only to be introduced to the fact that practicality often overrides dreams. The former wins out over the latter in all but the most magical of circumstances.

Not being one to brood, I revisited both of my lists and started making adjustments.

Now, I'm saying "I" in all of this not because Jeff didn't care what kind of house we bought,

but because he knew I would have to love it first and then he could be the final stamp of approval. As much as I wanted him to just agree with whatever I loved, that stamp of approval was the most important part. You see, I have "lost-dog syndrome" for houses, and we would've ended up an hour away from the boys' school in some dilapidated farmhouse with good bones if it had been entirely left up to me!

So, I revisited my lists, adjusted my date range in the search criteria, and started the hunt again. I purposed to apply one of the many lessons I have learned from years of restoring furniture: The most surprisingly wonderful pieces can often be found in the most unexpected places. With a renewed outlook, I began looking at any house that met the bare minimum requirements, and this time kept an open mind.

I'll give you one guess what kind of house we ended up buying. Yep, we ended up purchasing a very beige, suburban home. *With a two-story foyer!*

The reason we bought a home that didn't check every box on my wish list and, in fact, checked a few boxes on my deal-breaker list is that, unless you are single with an unlimited budget, purchasing a home isn't all about you and what you want. There is a variety of factors that have to be weighed, from commute times and school districts to budget and the kind of location that will suit your family's lifestyle. We had a pretty lofty list of needs and wants, and it became clear that I was the only one in my family who deemed the age of the house a significant sticking point.

So, we bought what I would consider to be an "upgraded builder-grade home." It still sported the builder-basic fixtures, the off-white and beige color scheme, and the wall-to-wall carpet.

Although, it clearly benefited from some generous extras, like a finished basement, built-in cabinetry, a sunroom addition, a split staircase, and crown molding added to some of the rooms. These features made it easy for me to forgive the fact that it wasn't the old farmhouse I dreamed of.

Before we moved into the house, I pored over pictures of it and dreamed about how I could make this house truly feel like home. In those early days of planning, I realized all the potential held in these walls. This house wasn't a fixer-upper. It didn't have major cosmetic flaws or dated design choices that needed to be undone. It was simply a sea of beige that needed an injection of character. It needed to be filled with the things that carry our stories, the colors, textures, and pieces that would make it feel like ours.

This is the third house Jeff and I have owned, and I learned something from the other two. Neither of them was love at first sight. Neither of them felt like home right away. In fact, we bought both of them because they were the best we could afford at the time. But when it was time to move on and sell each of them, I felt a deep affection for those houses that grew out of the work Jeff and I put into them as well as the life we lived there. I loved them because we made them our home.

The reality of your current house may have fallen short of your expectation, by an inch or by a mile, but I would encourage you to not judge the house too harshly for not living up to your dreams. Give it a chance to show its potential. Give it time to feel like home. Instead of pointing out the flaws, quirks, and unflattering design choices it may have been subjected to, approach your home with optimism and hope. Take a moment and listen to it.

The Art of Listening to *Your Home*

Listen to your house. I am not saying that your house and its contents have a soul and will speak audibly to you. (Before you think I'm totally crazy and find a decorating book that is more sensible, let me clarify that.) The house is a house. It's an inanimate object. But like a glove, it comes to life when a human inhabits it.

Whether you realize it or not, your home has taken on some of your personality, simply because you live in it. Your house brings some personality (and history) of its own to the table as well, though. Some homes are very outspoken and stubborn, engaging in a fiery debate with you. If you have one of those houses, you know just what I'm talking about! In contrast, there are homes that are mild mannered, agreeable, and easygoing, happily complying with your ideas and projects.

One of my friends, Suzanne, put it perfectly. She bought a 1700s manor house in Virginia and was restoring and furnishing it to use as an event and vacation rental. She was describing the decorating process to me over lunch one day and said, "If we put a piece of furniture in that house that it didn't like, it would just spit that piece of furniture right back out at us." She drew her head back and dramatically acted out spitting something across the room to make the point. The description evoked images of a chair being hurled out the front door, landing somewhere in the lawn, and I couldn't help but laugh. *That is a stubborn house.*

What Suzanne was really saying in that story

was that she was listening to the house and was willing to change a decision she made that wasn't working with its personality. It was picky and opinionated, just like an older woman who knows her mind after decades of experience. Suzanne embraced that, and I can tell you from seeing the home in person that the end result benefited from the collaboration.

So, how do you have a conversation with your house (and not feel like a lunatic in the process)? Well, you might feel like a lunatic, but just hang in there with me. This really is a valuable step, and I promise that you don't have to say anything out loud. Just get out a notepad, and take some time to really observe your house. While the focus of this book is on your tastes and preferences and what feels like home to you, the house, by

The tone and design of the ornate woodwork in this beautiful 1700s home dictated the scale and style of the furnishings and decor used in each room.

default, is a part of that equation. It's important to take time to recognize what the house is bringing to that equation so you can take advantage of the strengths that work for you and address the weaknesses that don't.

Let's start with these questions:

WHAT IS THE STYLE OF THIS HOUSE?

If you're not sure, let's try breaking style down into three categories:

1. **TRADITIONAL:** These homes are grounded in designs that are borrowed from older homes, like a four-square floor plan and central stair-case. This would include all colonials, Tudors, Victorians, and craftsman-, antebellum-, and farmhouse-style, etc.

2. **MODERN:** These homes are typically clean lined, geometric, and open concept. They are made of modern materials and have uncon-ventional floor plans and decorating elements. This category would include midcentury-modern, industrial, loft, and contemporary homes.

3. **COUNTRY:** These homes are quaint and gen-erally on the smaller side. Think dormers and sloped ceilings on the second story. This cate-gory includes cottages, Cape Cods, bungalows, and storybook-style homes.

Of course, some homes might bridge a couple of categories, like a 1980s ranch house that has a more modern floor plan but traditional design elements. There is also a myriad of home styles that I didn't name, because this would be a very long chapter if I tried to cover them all. Just do your best to define the style of your house.

The Noser family renovated this 1970s suburban home to look like a classic saltbox house.

WHICH CATEGORY DOES IT FIT IN BEST? WHAT STYLE WILL LOOK BEST IN THE HOUSE?

Think furnishings, colors, fabrics, finishing touches, architectural details, etc. Just because a home was built in the 1990s doesn't mean furniture stolen from the set of *Full House* is going to look best in it.

Maybe you have a nice collection of antiques and you moved into a contemporary-style home. You can still use antiques in a sleek and modern home, but you might choose to use furnishings that are industrial, clean-lined Shaker-style, or simple primitive pieces.

When we moved into our thirteen-year-old suburban home, I learned that the primitive pieces that worked so well in my 1940s Cape Cod didn't

Michael Wurm Jr.'s 1990s kitchen got a complete overhaul to blend modern convenience with the classic style of his 1950s suburban home.

fit in the more traditional style of our new house. Next to the two-story foyer, grand staircase, and nine-foot ceilings, the primitive pieces looked dinky and the chipping paint just looked grubby. My European antiques, though, the curvy French chairs and pine wardrobes, looked perfect, so I edited. I modified my style slightly to create a more cohesive relationship between the decor and the home.

HAVE ANY CHANGES BEEN MADE TO THE HOME, EITHER BY PREVIOUS OWNERS OR EVEN BY THE DESIGNER/ BUILDER THAT LOOK OUT OF PLACE?

If someone has lived in the house before you, chances are they injected their personal taste in some permanent or semipermanent way and now you've inherited it. It might be gleaming black granite floors that are too modern for a traditional foyer or damask wallpaper that is completely out of place in your mid-century modern home.

Sometimes these changes can distract from the true beauty and even the true style of a home. Identifying those out-of-character changes can often help you look past them and see the true potential of a space.

TAKE A MINUTE TO APPRECIATE YOUR HOUSE. WHAT ELEMENTS ALREADY FEEL LIKE HOME?

Set aside all of the potential in the house for just a minute and list all the things you appreciate about your home as it is right now. What elements already feel like home?

During the course of working on our suburban home, I came to realize I was approaching it with a bit of disappointment trailing along. While it is a beautiful house, it didn't really feel like our home. So, I was focused on what it wasn't and not everything that it was. I was selling this home short…misjudging it simply because it wasn't the old house I was dreaming about.

One of my blog readers wisely pointed out, "All old homes were once new."

When I looked at our home from that perspective, I was able to see all of the things this thirteen-year-old, well-built suburban home had in common with many things I love about old homes—transom windows above the doors, a back staircase, arched doorways, a "butler's pantry," and built-in furniture. Beyond that, it has high ceilings, beautiful light, a cleverly designed floor plan, and many other attractive qualities.

This house could be a great old home fifty or one hundred years down the road, and I get to be a part of that story, a part of building on the foundations of making it a great old home.

I started approaching the house with a new appreciation for what it was. It's not an old house and I don't need to try to make it look like one. It's not a farmhouse and I don't need to try to stuff it inside of that box. Doing that to this beautiful home, which can stand on its own two feet quite well, would be a disservice.

WHAT ARE FIVE AREAS WHERE THERE IS POTENTIAL FOR ADDING YOUR PERSONALITY AND CHARACTER?

Now you can make those lists of everything you want to do! How can you add some character and visual interest to your home? You don't need to list every project in every room (unless you want to), because that might be overwhelming. Just list five areas.

If you're not sure of specific projects you want to do, identify five places that are bare or lacking in personality, and I'll share loads of ideas for those as we get further along in this book.

WHAT FEELS LIKE HOME TO YOU?

I was initially going to ask you to try to identify your style here, but I realized that's the wrong question to ask. We are capable of liking and appreciating all sorts of styles, and I would argue that the true, authentic style of most people can't be succinctly defined. Typically, someone's personal style doesn't fit into a nice, neat category. It usually crosses over a few different categories and bends the rules. And it takes time, practice, and some self-awareness to develop. You have to start decorating, allowing lessons to be learned through trial and error, for your style to become evident.

Miles Davis, the legendary jazz musician, put it like this, "Sometimes you have to play a long time to be able to play like yourself." I originally heard this misquoted as "Sometimes it takes a long time to sound like yourself." Both sentiments are true. In this case, sometimes it takes practice to find your unique aesthetic voice. One of my artistic friends, Jeanne Oliver, says it this way: "You practice your way into your style."

I've been writing a decorating blog for almost ten years, have written hundreds of tutorials and articles about style for home magazines and websites, and I'm still not sure I can easily define my style! I like antiques, white ironstone china, European furniture, farmhouse primitives, and blue and white with splashes of green and warm wood tones. Basically, a combination of those good memories I shared earlier along with the memories I want to create.

When pinned down a few years ago to define my decorating style for an interview, I boiled it down to the phrase *French blue, farmhouse white*, but that's not the kind of answer you'll find in a style quiz. And I'm still not sure it fully encapsulates my style or what feels like home to me, but it's a stab at putting a few words to my personal decorating tastes and it's helped me stay true to that style as trends have come and gone.

What is more important than the specific style is this—*does it feel like home to you*? When each decorating decision is run through that filter, your authentic style has the opportunity to shine through.

So, let's skip the style quiz and try an exercise.

ONE: Write down some words that you would use to identify your style. As I did, write down what you like—furniture, colors, patterns, etc. Where do you like to shop? What catalog always entices you to flip through the pages? What TV shows and movies are more about the house than the story for you? It's okay if the list is short or if it fills up several pages. Writing it all down will (hopefully) bring out patterns.

TWO: Write down what home feels like to you. What are your best memories of home? What kinds of memories do you want to create? What kinds of things have you surrounded yourself with over the years? What does home smell like? What does it sound like? This list might be a close reflection of the home you grew up in, but it might have more to do with a place you stayed, a friend's house that you visited often and where you always felt welcome, or a vacation destination that was inexplicably familiar. It might be more about what you want home to feel like for your children or grandchildren. Sometimes what feels like home to us isn't easily explained. It just does.

THREE: Compare the two lists. Where do your preferences intersect with your idea of home?

This exercise can get you out of a style box that you or someone else may have put you in or you got into by following trends and style quizzes. My hope is these answers will allow you to simply love what you love, whether a particular style can be defined or not.

DOES YOUR CURRENT HOUSE FEEL LIKE HOME?

In the case of our suburban home, it didn't feel like home right away. There were so many choices that I would've made differently, and I felt that tension as we moved our things into the house. There was definitely a disconnect between the style of our furniture and accessories, all of the things we've collected and curated over the years, and the style of the house.

The positive thing in our case was that the disconnect was largely cosmetic and I knew that a lot of paint as well as some other customizations would be a bridge. I just needed to focus on the common ground.

So what about your house? Does it feel like home? Or does it feel like you're just parked there for a while until it's time to move on to the next place that will, hopefully, feel like home? If that's the case, don't wait! We can waste a lot of time waiting for the next thing that will be "perfect," searching for the greener grass. Let's work together on making that house, yes, *your house*, feel like your home.

great encouragement! It's sort of like intentionally searching for a few things you can admire or respect about a disagreeable person. When you ponder their good qualities, your opinion of them starts to improve.)

ARE YOU CURRENTLY WORKING WITH YOUR HOME OR FIGHTING AGAINST IT?

Fighting against the style of a home can be exhausting, and you often end up with parts of your home that look like your style and other parts that look distinctively different. It can feel disjointed and forced. And did I mention it's also exhausting? If you're approaching this book already feeling tired from that fight, take a deep breath.

My hope is that thinking through these questions will give you a new appreciation for your house so you can bring out the best and gently coax more of your style out of the areas that don't work for you. This should be a joy-filled journey, not a battle.

WHAT WOULD WORKING WITH YOUR HOME LOOK LIKE?

This is going to be different for everyone, but imagine shifting your focus from hiding what you don't like about your house to accentuating what you do like. What would that look like?

WHAT IS THE COMMON GROUND BETWEEN YOUR IDEA OF HOME AND THE STYLE OF THE HOUSE?

If you're dealing with that same tension that I felt moving into our current home, thinking through this question might help you out! Focus on where there are similarities between your house and what feels like home to you. Maybe they both have clean lines or a traditional feel. Perhaps commonality isn't found in a specific design element, but in the feelings they evoke. Maybe they are both whimsical or practical. Maybe it's the location—the mountains, or the beach, or sprawling farmlands, or a big sky that feels like home. Focus on the things that are right.

Finding those touch points can give you a great idea of what you can build on. (They can also be a

HOW CAN YOU BRING OUT THE BEST ASSETS OF YOUR HOME?

Even if it's just the light that streams into the windows in the evening or the flowering tree that shades the backyard or the layout. Discover the things you love, the things that are charming, unique, quirky, beautiful, and that feel homey. How can you make those shine?

WHAT IS YOUR HOUSE SAYING NOW THAT YOU ARE LISTENING?

Take some time to really think about this.

Be open.

Be observant.

Be hopeful.

Be an optimist.

Be a dreamer.

Be a student of your home.

Mistakes will be made, but mistakes are a part of the process. Look long-term. Allow these ideas to be more than just what you can accomplish in the next few weekends. What could your home look like in a year, five years, ten years? What projects will likely survive through decades of design trends? What customizations will make the most impact?

Listening to your house and appreciating it for what it is doesn't mean you don't make any changes, updates, modifications, or improvements. I would even argue that it does mean that, because all dynamic relationships require work. It doesn't mean the house needs to be architecturally preserved or restored to the way it looked the day it was built. It doesn't mean that your aesthetic voice is drowned out by 1980s brass fixtures and glossy oak cabinetry. You're welcome for that confirmation!

Listening to your house means that you are approaching it with an attitude of openness and comradery. You and your house are on the same team! This is not a battle of wills, you attempting to forcefully bend every stud and floorboard to your plan. If a house could express any human emotion, I'm sure it would express the desire to be cared for, even loved, and to be a shelter for many families through many years. (Remember, this is coming from someone who views any dilapidated house as one that should be adopted and cared for like a mangy puppy found by the side of the road.)

One thing that great old houses have in common, the ones that you sneak a picture of when you're walking through charming downtown areas and historic neighborhoods, is that they look like they have been well loved and cared for. The yards have been tended, and updates have been made with intention and respect. They exude this sort of quiet grace and confidence. *I've been here for one hundred years and I still look pretty darn good.*

So, make thoughtful changes that will help your house age well. Take a sledgehammer and knock down the wall that will let in more light, shed the popcorn ceiling, and paint the dark paneling. Rip out the carpet and remove the dated fixtures. Do it all for you *and the house*, working together to transform it into a beautiful, story-filled home for you and your family and all of the future families who will one day be lucky enough to live there.

CHAPTER II

TELLING YOUR STORY BY ADDING *character*

DECORATING IS AUTOBIOGRAPHY.
—GLORIA VANDERBILT

Home Is Where *You Fit*

I recently read, in Lydia Brownback's devotional *Contentment*, a simple and true definition of home: "Home is where you fit."

Why is it that a hospital room doesn't feel like home? Why is it that an office cubicle (even though we might spend the majority of our waking hours there and have pictures of our kids tacked up on the walls) doesn't feel like home? What is it that makes a hotel, even a luxurious one, not quite feel like home?

They may be charming and have character from an architectural standpoint. You may be cared for and comfortable. But those places rarely, if ever, have that magical combination of things that you select and arrange specifically to your tastes. That magical combination, more often than not, is found in the abundance of little details that all add up to make your home different from every other place on earth.

Simply put, it's where you fit.

What if the place where you're currently living doesn't feel like home? It's the best house you could afford. It was the house that was in the right location. It met most of the needs and a few of the wants. It's a beautiful house and may be *someone's* dream house, but it's not quite yours.

Remember that imaginary dream home we talked about at the very beginning of the book? Imagine that house once again. Why is it your dream house? Why does it feel like home to you? What color is it? What does it feel like in the summer? Or in winter? What are the design elements that make that house your dream home?

It's time to get specific. There are no restrictions and budget isn't an issue here—you're just daydreaming at this point.

What material are the kitchen counters? What style are the doorknobs? Are the bathroom faucets nickel or chrome or brass or black or bronze? How are the windows dressed? What kinds of plants and bushes line the front garden? What flooring material is used in each space? What colors are on the walls? What trims and moldings are found throughout the home? Is there wallpaper, exposed brick, beamed ceilings, an open staircase?

I could ask a thousand other questions, and I'm sure that if you've been through the home-building process, you've had to answer thousands of questions like those! The point of these questions isn't to overwhelm you or to get you thinking about all of the things you wish you had. (In fact, I'm all about loving the actual home you're in, and we'll dive into that in a later chapter.) The point of thinking about your ideal details of what home feels like to you is this: You actually can bring many of those elements into your current home!

Isn't that encouraging? You can bring bits and pieces of your ideal home to your current house to make it feel uniquely yours. By adding layers, creating strong focal points, making smart purchases, introducing a touch of the unexpected, and pulling it all together in the way that only you can, whatever you have to work with can become a beautiful, character-rich home that feels more like *your home* than you ever would have imagined.

Telling Your Story *Five Ways*

Think about one of your favorite things right now. It could be a food, a TV show, a piece of clothing. Got it? Think about why you love it. I'm guessing you can spout out a pretty decent list of why that thing is a favorite. *The TV show has deep stories, it makes me laugh, I've grown to care about the characters, etc. I love this shirt because it's flattering and comfortable, and I can wear it around the house, to work, or out to dinner.*

We are drawn to something, not for one reason, but for many reasons.

Now, I need you to lean in close, because I'm going to share a secret with you. Five secrets, actually. These are the secrets that take a space from *nice* to *wow, you did this?!* Just like your favorite ice cream, song, or movie, it's not one thing that makes it great. It's a collection of several things that, when you know how to combine them, create a unique space you and your family will love.

ONE: SELECT A STATEMENT PIECE

A statement piece is your muse. It's the thing that is the compass for the rest of the room. It's important to identify this first (or early in the process) so all future decisions can complement and support that statement piece.

Can a statement piece be anything? Yes! It can be anything that inspires you. However, there are a few important things to consider.

This stunning buffalo-check sectional was chosen to be a statement piece in an otherwise neutral living room.

YOU HAVE TO LOVE, LOVE IT *AND* IT HAS TO FEEL LIKE HOME TO YOU.

In my experience, a statement piece usually finds you more than you find it. It's the kind of thing you trip across in a late-night internet browsing session on Craigslist or you find when you hit an antique store at just the right time. Sometimes you already have the piece and you use it in an entirely new way that makes it noticeable and special. It's pure decorating magic when that happens! Whether you have it or shop for it, the piece should make you stop in your tracks. It should make your heart flutter and evoke strong positive feelings. It should make you irrationally paranoid that someone else is going to snap it up before you can get your hands on it.

    You have to *more* than love it. You have to *love* love it. If you're going to build a room around it and perhaps cause a lot of upheaval to give it the perfect place where it can be featured in your home, it has to fit into your idea of home, or it will always feel a little off.

    Follow your gut on these statement pieces. Typically, a statement piece will be a love-it-or-hate-it thing, so while I would advise you to listen to the opinion of your spouse, I wouldn't let other people talk you out of it. It's your statement—a representation of your idea of home and your decorating voice. It might be conventional, but it might be completely off-the-wall. Let it be. Embrace it. It's going in your home to be a feature, a point of conversation, and something that is unique.

    Select the piece with confidence and run with it.

IT SHOULD MAKE A STATEMENT.

This seems obvious, but we are trained to buy things for our home that are neutral or expected. When you browse furniture and home decor offerings online or in stores, a large percentage of what is available is beige, gray, white, and brown. It's inoffensive and quiet. It's meant to shrink into the background in the hopes that it will stay that way for at least a decade and won't look *d-a-t-e-d*. (I whispered that last word.)

    I feel this, too! We're so afraid of making the wrong decision or one that we'll be embarrassed about in five years that we settle for things that are commonplace, and safe. And I totally understand that.

An antique portrait in an ornate gold frame commands attention in the Nosers' formal living room.

A child-sized table that was once used in the Sunday school room of a church is now used as a place for puzzles, games, and coloring for the Dietzmans' grandchildren. Situated in front of the brick fireplace, it creates an inviting focal point in the open-concept family room, kitchen, and dining room.

Be safe with carpet. Go conservative with tile floors and countertops. Stay neutral with a sofa. *But don't do it with a statement piece.* And don't do it with any of those things I just mentioned if they are your statement piece! I decided to make my living room sofa a statement piece instead of a supporting piece of necessary furniture and ordered it in blue-and-cream buffalo check. It definitely makes a statement.

IT SHOULD BE TIMELESS.

I always enjoy looking at decorating books from ten, twenty, even thirty years ago to see what was in style and pick out the elements that I would still have in my home today. We can clearly see that harvest-gold appliances and powder-blue bathtubs were not timeless. We can also see that a shapely wing chair, though, won't ever go out of style.

I do think timelessness in decor is somewhat relative. I would encourage you to pick statement pieces for your home that are timeless *for you.* If you're a fellow lover of blue and white and have been for decades, sticking with that color palette will feel timeless for you. You can't ever imagine not loving blue and white. You might add accent colors here and there. You might branch out into a new color palette in a powder room or guest room. But when it comes down to what you love, you will always land in the same place.

If you are feeling a pull to another color palette, perhaps try it out in pillows and paint before you dive headfirst and invest in a statement piece that you might grow tired of in a few months.

If you don't have a statement piece for a room, that might be why you feel a little lost or the room feels a little lackluster and boring. I would suggest waiting until you figure out or find your statement piece before making too many other design choices. You can make some changes, like arranging the furniture, identifying the focal point, and working on the bones of the room, but don't get too far ahead of yourself.

TWO: IDENTIFY THE FOCAL POINT

Count yourself blessed when a room has an obvious and beautiful focal point, like a fireplace, a stunning ceiling treatment, picture windows overlooking an amazing view, or a wall of built-in cabinetry. Typically, there are one or two rooms in a home with a strong focal point—a formal room like a living or dining room and maybe the kitchen (because the cabinetry and appliances are built-in). The rest are boxes of drywall with closet doors and windows as the only thing visually breaking up the monotony of the four flat walls.

Adding a focal point to a room will immediately elevate the space. From a visual standpoint, it draws the eye, which emphasizes something you love and perhaps detracts from things that aren't finished or don't suit your style. It also gives you something to arrange the rest of the room around. For example, if there is a fireplace in a room, it gives a strong indication as to where the furniture in the room should be placed. It makes your other decorating decisions easier!

So what if you're starting with a room that is simply a box? A faux focal point can be added. Here are a few ideas to try.

FAUX FOCAL POINT

If you don't have an obvious architectural focal point, you can always create one. Add a salvaged fireplace mantel to a large, blank wall and style it just as you would if it were surrounding a built-in, functioning fireplace. Make this look even more convincing by painting the wall surrounded by the mantel black so it visually recedes, and arrange the furniture around it as if it were the real deal. If you treat it as an actual fireplace (minus the fires), guests might have to do a double take to see that it isn't.

You can also use this trick with mirrors that look like windows or nonfunctioning shutters or doors that lend an architectural point of interest to a room.

FURNITURE

Large-scale pieces of furniture are prime candidates to use as focal points in a space lacking one. Imposing bookcases, well-made beds, or a large hutch or buffet will stand in nicely. Just make sure the piece is large enough to command attention and to arrange other pieces of furniture around. There isn't a set size, but rather it is dictated by the scale of the room.

It's also important to pick a piece that fits your style and is interesting. If it's a bookcase, take time to style it thoughtfully, so it "says" what you want it to say. If it's a bed, select interesting linens and pillows, and pay attention to how the nightstands, lamps, and wall art frame it out. Just because the piece is big doesn't mean it should be the focal point. It should be special, too.

Assignment:
THE "TIMELESS TEST"

Look around your house and make a list of your very favorite things. It can be furniture pieces, fabric, dishes, art, or a paint color. Which ones have you loved and/or owned the longest? Those pieces can give you a good clue as to what feels timeless to you.

ART AND GALLERY WALLS

A large-scale piece of art can definitely qualify as a focal point in a room, but I would encourage you to think beyond traditional art. Some interesting alternatives are to hang a beautiful quilt, perhaps a family heirloom, an old pull-down map, a piece of architectural salvage, or even a small rug.

In lieu of one large piece, you can also hang a bunch of smaller items in a tight group, creating a gallery wall. Again, this doesn't have to include just pictures and flat art, but can incorporate clocks, baskets, textiles, etc. Grouping those smaller items together makes a bigger visual statement.

OPPOSITE: Two large pieces of furniture—an antique jelly cupboard and a primitive step-back hutch—act as focal points in a room without any defining architectural features.

A gallery wall composed of portraits and landscapes is a focal point in the corner of the Millers' living room.

Even the barest of bare-bones budgets can afford to add a focal point simply by painting one wall a striking, rich color. This is definitely an old decorating trick, but it has stuck around because it's inexpensive and effective.

Once you paint a wall a bold color, though, you need to treat it with importance. Put the largest piece of furniture on that wall or use it as a backdrop for a piece of art or a gallery wall. Color will draw the eye, so there needs to be something interesting to look at once it's there.

Color can also be used on a piece of furniture. If a traditional hutch, large dresser, cabinet, bookcase, or buffet is painted in a stunning, rich color, it can easily be transformed from blending into the background to making a statement.

THREE: BRING ON THE LAYERS

One of the best talents a gifted designer can bring to the table is the ability to confidently layer colors, patterns, and textures to make a room look polished, interesting, and cohesive. That doesn't mean the average person decorating their home isn't going to have an eye for mixing, matching, contrasting, and coordinating. It's just a learned skill that might need to be developed and nurtured with practice. It also might mean some trial and error as your skill is honed and refined.

The most beautiful, interesting rooms are ones that have a lot of layers happening, like a deep character in a good story. Layers can be dramatic, full-on contrasting colors and patterns, or they can be subtle and monochromatic.

The good news is that there are some general decorating guidelines that can point you in the right direction until you become more confident to start breaking some rules. There is also a myriad of resources available to help you mix and match. Companies create cohesive collections for that very reason, and it's okay to use those curated colors, patterns, and textures as a starting point.

Assignment: FIND THE FOCUS

Walk into each room in your house and determine the focal point (if there is one). First of all, do you love that focal point? If so, are you featuring it? If not, what can you do to change it or make it better? Could you shift the focus to something else that you do love?

If the room doesn't have a focal point, how can you add one? Write down at least one idea for each room.

COLOR, PATTERN, TEXTURE: THE LAYERING TRIFECTA

The three most important decorating elements to keep in mind as you're adding layers to a room are color, pattern, and texture.

What colors can you pull out of your statement piece to use in other places in the room? What color should be dominant? What color or colors should be accents? Do you want the colors to be high contrast or softer, more monochromatic?

What patterns will come into play in the room? Do you want to contrast the style of the statement piece, playing with juxtaposition? Or do you want the room to feel more traditional and cohesive?

What do you want the textures to say about this room? Is it cozy and casual? Is it formal and luxurious? Are there creative places you can add texture? Where can you add textural variety and contrasts?

Those are a lot of questions to consider! Creating a living mood board is a fantastic way to take all of these overwhelming options and simplify them visually.

WHAT IS YOUR PREFERRED COLOR PALETTE?

Let me start off by stating that color is complicated! If you find yourself overwhelmed with color, there is good reason. Color is subjective and it changes with the light as well as environment. A color that looks fantastic in one room might look off in the next. It is tricky even for those well versed in its complexities. If you ever loved a swatch, painted your entire room in it, and then hated it…well, you're a part of a very large (and I'm sure growing) club.

I also need to say that there aren't good colors or bad colors. There are only colors that you like and ones that you don't. This is typically something that's intuitive, whether you realize it or not. There are colors that you will gravitate toward and some you will be averse to. Your preference for colors can be swayed, though, by what you see regularly. You might find yourself following trends or selecting colors predominately used in homes that you love. Just as it is with decorating style, it's easy to get distracted and lose sight of what *you* really love, what you would choose on your own without influence.

Early in my blogging years, aquas, teals, and watery blues were in. I remember poring over blogs featuring homes in these colors, and I decided to use them in my master bedroom. I painted the walls a soft blue and found toile fabric featuring all of the trendy colors. After decking out the room in these shades and living with it for a couple of years, I realized it wasn't me at all! How did I get pushed away from my favorite palette of French blues, indigo, and creamy whites? I saw beauty, admired it, and wanted to replicate

COLOUR IS A CONSTANT CREATIVE DECEIVER, A SORT OF HUMOROUS AND SCIENTIFIC MAGICIAN.
—*PHILIPPA STANTON,*
CONSCIOUS CREATIVITY: LOOK, CONNECT, CREATE

it. Instead of using the images that inspired me as a springboard, I used them as a blueprint. I didn't ask important questions about what I loved and what felt timeless to me.

I feature a lot of blues, whites, and greens in this book, because that is the color palette I love and use throughout my home, predominately in my paintings and design work, and even in my

Assignment: PLAY WITH COLOR

Go to the paint store and grab any chips and swatches that catch your eye. Cut out the specific chips that you like (they are usually on a card with three to five other colors) and move them around on a table. Which combinations do you love? Try pairing the color chips with fabrics, textiles, flooring, etc. and see what works. What color could be the walls? What color could be used as an accent on a piece of furniture?

You don't have to use all of the colors or even any of them, but establishing some combinations you like could be a starting point as you view them against your statement piece and fabrics you want to use in the room. Take a picture of the combinations you like best, or staple or clip them into a notebook to use as a reference.

wardrobe. But if you love reds, earth tones, or pastels, don't let me sway you away from that! Go with your intuition, even if it's not what's trending.

The first question I would ask you about color is: *Do you like warm or cool colors?* Most suburban homes tend to have a warm color palette. You'll find lots of warm beiges, browns, creams, and taupes. This was the case with the home we purchased in Minnesota and, since I like a cool color palette, I knew immediately that I wanted to change the painted surfaces and finishes in order to shift the color temperature of the house. The warm, peachy white that was used on all of the walls and trims looked almost dingy against my cooler greens and blues.

If you like cool colors as I do, it doesn't mean that you can't use any warm colors or finishes in your home. I love mixing in warmth through natural materials like woven baskets, wood that glows with the patina of age, leather-bound books, and creamy whites in antique textiles. It adds warmth and coziness to the cool blue-gray walls and bright white trim.

The second question I would ask about color is: *What saturation level do you like?* Saturation refers to the brilliance or intensity of the color. Primary colors are intense. Soft earth tones and pastels are less saturated and therefore softer to the eye. Again, there isn't a right or wrong answer to this question, just what you like. I will go out on a limb and say that most interiors use less saturated colors that are muted and toned, but there are certainly exceptions to this.

I would say that the more intense the color, the trickier it can be to use in a home. Bold colors can be used, but they take a bit more finesse. Saturation is particularly important when selecting wall colors. In a little paint chip, a yellow might look cheery and bright, but it looks garish when on an entire wall. An orange appears warm and cozy, but it looks like you color matched a caution cone

TIPS ON SHOPPING FOR FABRIC

I am a fabric hound. If I see a fabric I like, I will sniff it out, track it, and hunt it down. I will dig in the resource sections of books, follow brand tags, comb websites, and send inquiries to find out the name of the pattern. Once I have the name of the pattern and the maker, I will run a good ole Google search to see where it is for sale. This means that I don't buy from one specific website when shopping for fabrics, but I buy from whichever site has the best deal. This shopping method can lead me off the beaten path, which is the best place to find unique pieces.

1. DO LOTS OF SEARCHES! Typically, if you describe the fabric you're looking for in a search engine box, you're going to find it or similar fabrics that you might like more or might be more affordable. When I'm working on a room, I spend a lot of time searching for fabrics until I find exactly what I imagine for the room.

2. ORDER SAMPLES! Getting your hands on fabric samples is key, and I order a lot of them. Sometimes they are free and sometimes they cost one to five dollars, depending on the company and size of the fabric swatch. I don't always order them with the intention of buying that specific fabric, but more to test out color, pattern, and scale to see what I like and what works. Some of the samples I use are even from decorators' swatch books that I order off Etsy, and the patterns might not even be made anymore. If you don't want to purchase fabric swatches, print up a picture of the fabrics, and experiment with them that way. Just keep in mind that your printer might not accurately match the true fabric colors.

3. ASK ABOUT ORDERING FABRIC BY THE YARD. Do it even if that's not an option on the website. I fell in love with a green velvet fabric from Arhaus when I was looking at swatches for the living room sectional. I ended up going with the large-scale blue-and-cream check, but I inquired about ordering the green fabric by the yard to make pillows, and I was able to purchase it through special order.

4. LOOK FOR BOLTS OF FABRIC IN UNEXPECTED PLACES. I've bought fabric from all over the place, including the trunk of someone's car! I've bought it at yard sales, thrift stores, antique shops, and flea markets. Just keep your eyes open for folded stacks or rolls. You can often find great bargains shopping this way. I also love mixing in vintage, antique, and out-of-print fabrics from Etsy and eBay.

5. SHOP WITH A HIGH-LOW APPROACH. My fabrics can be anywhere from free to more than one hundred dollars per yard, so it's a pretty wide range! I use expensive fabric very sparingly for pillows and small details and use inexpensive fabrics for larger projects. Most of the fabrics I use are between fifteen and thirty dollars per yard, supplemented with ones that are five to ten dollars per yard. I look for sales and coupon codes and always compare prices. Fabrics can be a luxurious part of a room, adding texture, pattern, and color, so it's a smart place to splurge in small quantities.

When I can't make a decision on a little fabric swatch, I'll usually order one yard or a half yard as long as the fabric isn't too expensive. This allows me to wrap the fabric around pillows or tack it up on the wall to get a sense of how I like it in the room. Any kind of visual you can give yourself is going to be helpful (and worth the expense) when you're making decisions.

Assignment:
LIVING MOOD BOARD

Create a living mood board for one room in your house that feels unfinished. Clip and print pictures of inspiration rooms and pieces. Incorporate a variety of paint chips and fabric swatches, and play with them until you find a combination you love. Add accessories, trim, items collected from nature, etc. until you have a cohesive design concept.

considering and brush them either on the wall or on a sample board that can be tacked to the wall. Colors can look dramatically different from one room to the next, so you can't always trust what's worked for you in the past.

MIXING AND MATCHING FABRICS

In my opinion, coordinating fabrics is one of the hardest things to do when pulling together a room! Fabrics bring in color, pattern, and texture, and all three of those elements need to play well with one another. To compound the problem, there are millions of fabrics to choose from to mix and match, and your upholstered furniture is already bringing some kind of textile to the table. So where do you even start?

First of all, the more firsthand experience you can acquire with mixing and matching patterns, the better you will be at it. (We talk more about "practicing decorating" on pages 272–276.) While I would encourage you to dig elbow-deep in a remnant bin and play with all of the colors, patterns, and textures you can, I'm going to offer you a shortcut! Here is what I've learned playing with fabrics over the years:

SCALE: Pick one large-scale pattern, one medium, and one small.

PATTERN: Select one allover, flowing pattern, like a floral, paisley, damask, or toile; one geometric, like a stripe, plaid, check, or polka dot; and one solid.

COLORS: Stick with a color family that compliments your statement piece (which might even be

when it's rolled on and dry. A good rule of thumb when selecting paint chips for interiors is to stay away from the "middle of the deck," which is typically populated with bright, saturated colors. Stick with the ends of the deck, which usually house collections of neutrals and colors curated for decorating.

Once you've established the basics of your color preferences, it's easier to narrow down the colors you want to use in your home. From there, it's just a matter of playing with color combinations to see what you love, what feels like home to you and matches your personality.

A word of warning: Do not buy paint until you have your fabrics picked out. Pick up as many chips as you want, but it can be hard to match fabric to a specific color that's already on the wall. Matching paint to a fabric is much easier. And always purchase a sample pot of the colors you're

TELLING YOUR STORY BY ADDING CHARACTER

a fabric). If you have difficulty matching colors, stick with two colors and a neutral—beige or brown, black or dark gray, or white or cream. For example, my favorite color palette is blue, green, and white. Giving myself clear boundaries helps me say an immediate no to fabrics that are outside of the self-imposed boundaries.

TEXTURE: Select at least two different textures to keep things visually interesting. Keep in mind where the fabric will be used so it's fitting for the application. You want pillows to be soft, upholstery to be durable, curtains to have a nice drape, etc.

CREATE A LIVING MOOD BOARD

Mood boards made of magazine clippings or created online can provide a beneficial visual of how furniture, fabrics, and paint colors can relate to one another, but nothing will be as valuable as having physical samples collected and arranged together. Most websites will send a certain number of free samples for fabric, paint, wallpaper, counters, tile, flooring, and even wood and painted finish options for cabinetry, furniture, blinds and shutters, etc.

If you can't get a specific sample, paint out your own swatches or use items you already have that will lend the same feel. Creating this living mood board accomplishes a few things. First of all, you have the opportunity to see the actual colors, textures, and patterns in the room where they will be used. You can watch how the light changes and affects the look of each choice. You also have the chance to live with the mood board for as long as you need to in order to make up your mind or to make the necessary changes.

When you are working on a room, it's easy to get antsy to buy something. Concentrating on creating the living mood board will force some patience and help you make stronger decorating decisions in the end. (And your budget will appreciate it, too!)

INCORPORATE LAYERS ONE AT A TIME

The living mood board will help a lot when it comes to experimenting with colors, patterns, and textures. With free squares of fabrics and swatches of paint, you can try as many combinations as you want until you find the one that speaks to you.

Even with a well-planned mood board, there is still the possibility of a decision not working successfully in actuality. For this reason, I would suggest adding one layer at a time. Start with a rug or another statement investment piece that you love, then buy that piece of furniture or piece of art you had sitting in your online shopping cart. Taking the makeover one step at a time will give you a chance to back out of a decision or shift gears if it doesn't look the way you imagined.

This is your home, not a home makeover television show—you don't have to get everything in place in forty-eight hours! There is no reason to move forward with a pit in your stomach doubling down on a decision you already regret simply because you feel like it's too late.

Slow and steady will win the decor race every time!

FOUR: SHOW OFF YOUR PERSONALITY THROUGH FINISHING TOUCHES

While this part seems like it should be the easiest, this is where a lot of people hit a wall of decision fatigue, feel lost, or question their taste. But this is the part of the room that isn't about what other people like, or what's trendy and popular. It's about what you love and what feels like home to you. And adding personality is a dynamic, endless process. As you grow and change, so can the personality you lend to your home. Knowing these decisions aren't permanent or final can take some of the pressure off.

A dear friend of mine, Shaunna, coined one of my favorite sayings about minimizing anxiety over decorating decisions (and you have to imagine this in a lovely Southern drawl), "Spackle dries in, like, three minutes." This was her response when a decorating client was feeling angst about hanging a picture on a wall, and I've imagined those words repeatedly when I'm scooting around furniture or rearranging a bookshelf and feeling unsure about it. It's just paint, just a nail hole, just some books, just a chair that can be moved again. These are decisions I like right now and it's okay if I don't like them down the road. I can like them and enjoy them until I'm ready to change them.

So let this be the fun part! Follow your gut. Use the pieces that make you smile and arrange them in a way that serves you and gives you a lift when you see them. Put on some good music and experiment. We talk a lot more about finishing touches and styling accessories in chapter X, so if you're ready to get to work on this step, jump over to page 247.

FIVE: ADD THE UNEXPECTED

For some, the idea of trying out unconventional or off-the-wall ideas is easy and exciting. For others, it's very uncomfortable! I'm not trying to push you into any decorating style that doesn't feel authentic and beautiful to you. If you don't like anything that is unexpected, that's okay.

I would challenge you, though, to try pushing *one* boundary of your style. It can be as simple as injecting a little wink and a nod with a humorous accessory or bringing in a surprising color with one throw pillow. Adding something that's unexpected or even using something traditional in an unexpected way immediately sparks conversation: *There's probably a story behind this...* It can be big and bold, or it can be subtle, but I guarantee that it will make your room unique and more interesting!

I purchased an antique oak hutch at a flea market a few years ago. The hardware was mismatched and didn't do much for the piece, so I was going to replace it with some pulls that were appropriate for the era of the hutch. There would've been nothing wrong with that, but as I was digging through my hardware stash, my mom spotted some brass pulls shaped like barn swallows in flight. Now, she is about as traditional as they come when it comes to decor, but she suggested I give them a try. That small, unexpected addition to the hutch ended up making the piece.

One of my boundaries was pushed, and the result was better than if I'd just played it safe.

As a quick recap, here are the five steps to creating a room that is uniquely yours:

1. SELECT A STATEMENT PIECE.
2. IDENTIFY THE FOCAL POINT.
3. BRING ON THE LAYERS.
4. SHOW OFF YOUR PERSONALITY.
5. ADD THE UNEXPECTED.

While I think the order of these steps is a progression that makes sense, they don't have to be done in this order. The typical scenario is most likely about reworking a room instead of starting with an empty space. Always start with what you have and work from there. You might be able to establish a focal point before you have a statement piece selected. There may be a clear vision for how you want to show some personality, but you're stuck on colors and fabrics.

Each room is going to fall into place in a slightly different way, and it might not be perfectly in order. Don't let the order stress you out. Instead, focus on making intentional decisions that build on and support your previous decisions.

As you work on bringing character to your home, make sure it's *your* character, *your* story. Be honest about what you love, and try not to be swayed by passing trends and the dominating decorative aesthetic of the day.

A home can have the perfect combination of components to look beautiful for pictures on social media, but if it's not a fit for you, it won't feel like home. It won't feel like the perfect fit.

Assignment:
GET OUT OF YOUR BOX

Try adding one unexpected element to one room in your house and live with it for one week. If you're not sure about it, take a picture of that unexpected decision in the context of the room and see how it looks on a screen. It's interesting how viewing our room through a picture can help us have a fresh set of eyes. If you don't like it, try something different. If trying new things is out of your comfort zone, it might take some practice (or a good creative friend) to hit on something that really works. Once you have one victory, though, you'll have the confidence to get even more creative with your ideas.

CHAPTER III

LIVING
spaces

liv·ing	space (place)
/'liviNG/	/spās/
noun	*noun*
the pursuit of a lifestyle of the specified type	buildings or areas used for a specified purpose or activity

THE BEST ROOMS HAVE SOMETHING TO SAY ABOUT THE PEOPLE WHO LIVE IN THEM.
—DAVID HICKS

The Pursuit of a *Lifestyle*

I love the definition I found for "living": "the pursuit of a lifestyle of the specified type." The example given alongside this particular definition was "the benefits of a country living." What if we approached our living spaces with that mindset? It's not just about putting a sofa in the spot that has the best view of the TV, but it's making all of the decorating choices in pursuit of a specific lifestyle. I'm a little nerdy and enthusiastic when it comes to decorating, so this idea is exciting to me! When there is intention behind our decisions for a room, they transform what might be superficial and materialistic into an endeavor that has depth and meaning. We're not just addressing how a room looks, but we're addressing the life we want to live in that room. We're defining or perhaps redefining our idea of what home feels like.

How does this idea translate into how you approach decorating the room?

Seating is the most obvious need in the room. If you've ever moved into a house and lived a few days without furniture, you know that somewhere to sit is greatly missed when absent! Beyond the basic need for seating, this is a key place to consider the lifestyle you want. When you imagine your family in this room over the years, what is the picture you see? Are you playing board games? Having conversations about heartbreak and celebrating milestones? Curling up for a family movie night? Maybe a little bit of all of these and more?

When considering how the room will be used, the furniture pieces and layout need to facilitate those activities. A solitary couch isn't going to be conducive to conversation. A grouping of stiff and uncomfortable chairs might work for visiting with guests over an evening but won't be ideal for snuggly movie nights and sick days on the sofa.

The seating is the anchor of a living room, so getting the chairs, sofas, sectionals, and love seats right will help everything else from lighting to tables to rugs fall into place.

Take a few minutes to write a brief story of the life that will be lived in this room. I know this might stretch some of you! This doesn't have to be a great work of literature. It can be bullet points and simple ideas. "Every Friday, the four of us gathered together, ate pizza, and alternated picking the movie we would watch. Sunday afternoons, we played board games together, then Dad took a nap on the sofa. We set up the Christmas tree in that corner and would often sit in the evenings to enjoy the lights. The boys played chess and cards on that game table in the corner and built a fort on snow days with the sofa cushions. Every year, we pulled extra chairs in from the dining room when extended family came for Thanksgiving and Easter." Etc.

I know this sounds a bit like a middle school creative writing assignment, but it really is helpful when it comes to decorating a room. When you tell the story of the life you want to live there to yourself, the picture of the furniture you need in that room and how it could best be arranged becomes clearer. It's like going to the grocery store with a recipe in mind instead of buying a bunch of random ingredients that could make a dinner. It's easier to avoid settling into a default furniture

arrangement in favor of an intentional one. There still might be a trial-and-error component and a slow evolution that occurs, but it gives you a good starting point.

Knowing what won't work will narrow the options for what will work. The story will tell you that you need two chairs flanking the fireplace, facing a sofa or a sectional in the corner with a pair of swivel chairs on the opposite side of the room. It will tell you if you need occasional chairs, stools, or ottomans for extra seating, tables for drinks and games, task lighting or ambient lighting.

FURNITURE ARRANGING (AND REARRANGING)

So, what if you're not starting from scratch in your room? You already have furniture in the space, and some of it obviously fits with that story while some doesn't. I would suggest starting with what you have. Looking at your living space in a fresh way will most likely give you a new perspective on your existing pieces. You can either start scooting furniture around or try this exercise—playing paper dolls with your house. You can even break out the colored pencils if you're so inclined!

While you're arranging and rearranging your furniture (in your head, on paper, or in actuality), it's important to keep in mind what the focal point or points will be in the room as well as the traffic paths.

SETTING THE STAGE

It might seem like the stage should be set before the room is populated with furniture, but I deliberately put this section after, because I believe, unless you have a very clear vision, you have to live in a room for a while before you want to make more permanent changes to the floor, walls, ceiling, and focal points. You might discover that you don't use the fireplace at all, and that the furniture arrangement would be much better for your lifestyle if you remove it. Your initial thought is to remove the carpet, but you realize your kids are always wrestling on the floor and it might be better to wait on the wood floors until they are past that phase.

As we talked about in chapter I, it's also a good idea to take some time to listen to the house. What's working and what's not? Again, unless you have a crystal-clear vision, rushing into

Assignment:
REARRANGE YOUR ROOM ON PAPER

Buy graph paper and architectural templates to draw out furniture pieces. Draw out your room to scale on the graph paper, and draw and cut out pieces of your furniture using the templates. (You can also find furniture templates online.) Then play with your room! You can even make other cutouts of furniture pieces from other rooms in the house or that you would consider purchasing that would fit nicely into the story of the life you want to live in that room. If you want to try this idea on a living scale, measure the furniture and tape out the footprint of each piece on the floor and even the walls. This simple exercise can give you new ideas, a project list, a shopping list, and a clear direction before you move any furniture or spend any money.

wallpaper or building a new mantel might be an expensive or time-consuming regret. Patience is the best prevention for most decorating mistakes. Not all, but most. So, it's worth taking the time to get the function of the room right first.

Setting the stage is all about addressing the bones of the room to support the life you want to live in that space. These elements are primarily decorative but can have an impact on the way the room feels and functions. These elements include the flooring, wall paint or treatment, lighting, and architectural elements like trim, molding,

windows, doors, fireplaces, and built-in shelving. A good place to start is to remove anything that isn't working with the house, with your style, or both.

The very day we moved into our 1940s Cape Cod in a small town in Pennsylvania, we ripped out Berber carpeting that covered original oak floors in the old part of the house. We didn't need time to listen to the space or observe our life there. We knew we preferred hardwood over dark and dated carpeting, so it came out before the sun set on the house becoming ours. It didn't serve the house or our style.

The original pinewood trim was a different story. I was pretty sure I wanted to paint it, but I needed to live with it for a while to be sure. I changed other elements in the room before I decided to prime and paint the trim, a decision not easily undone if I change my mind!

Once you've removed items that aren't working, take some time to live in the edited space. Change can usually be jarring, and it takes a few days to adjust. I've learned not to rush from one big change to the next. I'll take at least a few days before making another decision. For example, when light reflects off of a wood floor, it reflects the tone of the floor onto the walls. In the case of my living room, birch floors cast a warm, yellow glow, making my gray-blue walls lean blue-green. Taking time to observe the tones of a new wood floor can help you select a paint color that works with those cast tones.

ADDING ARCHITECTURAL INTEREST

Perhaps other than paint, trim is one of the best ways to add depth and character to a boring room. In a weekend, beadboard can be installed on walls or ceilings for an instant cottage vibe. Board-and-batten is the perfect treatment to achieve a craftsman style, and shiplap or tongue-and-groove boards immediately lend a farmhouse feel to any space.

OPPOSITE: Three-quarter-height wainscoting in a historic design was installed in a 2000s addition in this 1940s home to give it character.

SCALE AND PROPORTION

Other than the style of the trim, scale and proportion are the most important things to consider when either assessing existing trims and moldings or adding new ones. I have seen so many "great rooms" in suburban homes with lofty ceilings and oversized windows that have only dinky 2" baseboards installed around the room or a tiny mantel that looks even smaller in relation to the scale of the room. For a room to look polished and the design to look intentional, installing architectural detail proportional to the space and fitting for the house is critical.

WHAT STYLE OF TRIM IS RIGHT FOR YOU AND YOUR HOME?

When selecting trim, you do want to consider your own design style, but it's much more important to consider what will work well with the style of the house. It's a semipermanent addition and will ultimately look better if it complements the style of the house instead of detracting from it or competing with it. This doesn't mean you have to do fussy, over-the-top trim that you don't like simply because your house has a more formal feel, but you might want to consider simple yet traditional moldings as opposed to treatments that would be too modern or casual.

This is particularly important in public spaces that are open and visible to other rooms. In a private space, like a bedroom or bathroom, there can be a greater departure from the overall style of the house.

For example, I wanted our laundry room to have more of a cottage feel, even though our house is clearly not a cottage. Beadboard seemed like an appropriate wall treatment for a laundry room, though, and it's visible only from the kitchen. So I installed it on all of the walls and gave the laminate cabinets a makeover (more on that later), and it completely transformed the feel of the space yet didn't feel out of place in a traditional-style suburban home. It works.

Assignment:
"WINDOW-SHOPPING" FOR TRIM

Take a field trip to the hardware store and spend some time browsing through the trims and molding. Look at molding for doorframes, windows, chair rails, and baseboards, crown moldings, and every other type of trim. What do you gravitate toward? Do you like a simple profile or one that's more ornate? Do you like graceful curves or straighter lines? How could various trims be used to add architectural interest to your home? Take pictures and make notes to reference when you're back at home. Trips through the trim aisle almost always kick-start a few ideas for me!

Project: PICTURE FRAME MOLDING

I am a fan of adding trim to a big box of a room to make it look special, important, and higher quality. Almost any kind of architectural interest will do that. Chair rail is very simple to install and a lightning-fast project. Adding picture frame molding will make it even more interesting and is still quick and inexpensive. It's a good weekend project and will cost an average of $150–$200 depending on the size of the room and wood you select.

WHAT YOU'LL NEED

- Chair rail and trim (You can purchase both of these pre-primed, which is helpful if you intend to paint them.)
- Measuring tape
- Pencil
- Level
- Miter saw
- Finish nailer (You can use a hammer and finishing nails, but that will take much longer!)
- 1½" finishing nails
- Interior, paintable trim caulk
- Caulk gun
- Paper towels or rags
- Primer
- Paint
- 2½" angled sash brush
- Paint roller
- 4" or 6" microfiber roller cover
- Paint tray
- Drop cloth
- Safety gear—eye and ear protection for when using the saw

A FEW HELPFUL TIPS

- The trim typically comes in 16' lengths, and if you're getting a lot (we needed 230' for our living room and guest room), it's worth having the store cut it down for you as opposed to using the manual saw on the cutting table that customers can use. We would've been there for an hour cutting all of the pieces. We had them cut into 8' lengths so we could fit them in my van.
- Take the time to measure the space and draw a clear diagram for how you want to configure the boxes of the picture frame molding. Instead of making the boxes uniform sizes, I opted for a 3" uniform border around each box. If the span of one wall was over 50", I would add two or three boxes to add more interest.
- To determine the height of each box, I took the measurement from the top of the baseboard to the bottom of the chair rail and subtracted 6" (3" for the space on the top and 3" for the bottom). This was the measurement for the vertical trim pieces. For the horizontal pieces, I measured the total width of one wall and subtracted 6" as well. If I wanted to add two or three boxes, I would subtract 9" for two (3" for each side and 3" for the middle) or 12" for three.
- Under the windows of each room, I had the trim line up with the window frame exactly. Having those boxes inset 3" on each side would've looked a little strange in my opinion.

STEPS

1. INSTALL THE CHAIR RAIL. A chair rail can be any height you want, but about 32" from the floor for 9' ceilings is pretty standard. Use a measuring tape and a level to mark the wall at the desired height. Use a miter saw to cut the chair rail to length (it may require butting two or more pieces together), mitering the ends when applicable. Line the bottom of the chair rail up to the marked line and attach it to the wall using a finish nailer and nails.

2. CUT THE TRIM PIECES. Cut the vertical and horizontal pieces to the measurements on your diagram. Since these pieces are forming a box, each corner will be mitered at a forty-five-degree angle. I would suggest double-checking the first few cuts to ensure your diagram is correct! Because measuring with a measuring tape can be unreliable, measure and cut one piece and then use it as a template for the others of the same size. That way, the pieces are exactly the same and the box will be perfectly square and not off by $1/16$" here or there.

3. INSTALL THE TRIM. Cut two 3" blocks of scrap wood to use as a measuring tool for installing the trim. This way, you won't have to pull out the measuring tape and level with each piece you're installing. Just position one or two of the blocks against the chair rail, base molding, corner of the wall, or door or window casing to determine the proper spacing. Because not all trim, floors, and walls are level and plumb, use the blocks as a guide. Double-check against a small level, especially if something looks off. Start with the top horizontal piece, then add the right-hand piece, double-checking it with a level. Fit the bottom and left pieces at the same time, to make sure the corners line up nicely. (This is where it's very helpful to have a second set of hands!)

4. CAULK, PRIME, AND PAINT. Caulk is magic! It will fill any gaps, holes, and cracks. Apply it in a thin bead with a caulk gun. Wipe with a damp paper towel or rag to smooth. Repeat this process on all visible seams and holes made by nails. Apply a quality primer once the caulk is dry, followed by one or two coats of satin, semigloss, or gloss paint. (See pages 220–229 for more tips on paint and painting.)

Project: BOX BEAMS

The ceiling is often referred to as the "fifth wall" in the decorating world, and it is definitely the most neglected "wall." If your ceilings are high or you feel like your room needs more visual importance, beams are the perfect way to add some interest without getting into major construction projects.

In our living room, we created a faux coffer ceiling with beams and molding, but we could've just opted for three straight beams. Select a beam style and layout that suits your room and the style of the home.

While most of the projects in this book are well suited to DIY beginners, this project is for those who have intermediate building experience or who can work alongside someone with intermediate-to-advanced building knowledge. There are some great alternatives to building your own beams available on the market. Faux wood and premade beams are easier to install but are generally more expensive. They are also more style specific and have fewer options to customize, but if you can find one that works well for your decorating taste, it can be a good alternative to building your own from scratch.

....

WHAT YOU'LL NEED

- Measuring tape
- Stud finder
- Ladder (It's helpful to have two.)
- Chalk line and chalk (or laser level)
- Miter saw
- 2" × 6" boards (These are the support boards, so they will not be visible. Just make sure they are as straight as possible.)
- 1" × 6" boards (These will make up the finished boxes, so they should be a premium wood.)
- Painter's tape
- Crown molding or trim
- Drill and drill bits
- 3½" self-tapping wood screws
- Heavy-duty wall anchors

- Pliers or wire clippers
- Finish nailer
- 1¾" finishing nails
- Caulk and caulk gun
- Primer
- Quality trim paint
- Paint brush (2" or 2½" angled sash)
- Paint roller
- Roller cover (I used a 6" microfiber roller cover.)
- Roller tray
- Drop cloth
- Safety gear—eye and ear protection for when using the saw and a dust mask for sanding

A FEW HELPFUL TIPS

- Draw out a detailed plan before you start in order to create a shopping list and cut list. Take into account where the joists are in your ceiling to make sure the beams are securely installed.
- You will be installing long pieces of wood, so this a two-person job.
- When you are installing things overhead, it's always best to err on the side of overkill! You should be able to hang from these beams, not feel like they could fall if someone doesn't tiptoe in the room above. Use long, quality screws inserted into joists or several heavy-duty wall anchors when joists aren't present above a particular beam. You may even want to consider a different design to make sure all beams are installed into joists.
- Never walk away from a beam that is just nailed in to keep it from shifting. Immediately insert screws to secure the beam in place.
- Prime and paint the beams and molding before installing them. The paint will need some touch-up after they're installed, but it will greatly reduce the amount of time you have to work overhead.
- If you're going to stain your beams, make sure to use quality, stain-grade wood and wood fillers.
- The ceiling between the beams can be filled with tongue and groove, beadboard, shiplap, or some other kind of wood treatment to add even more texture and interest.
- While I painted my beams white, they would've looked striking in a color as well.
- Ceilings and walls are rarely plumb, level, or perfectly flat. There will likely be gaps created by an uneven ceiling, even in new, well-built homes. Just roll with it! Caulk and trim can cover a lot, and it doesn't have to be perfect.

STEPS

1. Use a stud finder to locate the joists, and mark them on the ceiling where the beams will be installed. For beams that are running perpendicular to the joists, a screw or two can be inserted at each mark into the joists to securely support the beam. This will also show if beams running parallel to the joists line up with the joists or if wall anchors will need to be used.

2. Based on your plan and position of joists, measure and mark the desired place to install each beam. Snap a chalk line between the marks to create a perfectly straight line where each beam will be installed.

3. Mark the center point (lengthwise) of each 2" × 6" board so they can be lined up with the chalk lines. Cut boards to size, if necessary. Hold one board up to the ceiling, lining it up with the chalk line. Nail it into place with a finish nailer to hold it steady until screws are inserted. Immediately insert self-tapping screws through the board into the joists. Continue installing boards in this manner, perpendicular to the joists and then parallel. Leave a 1" gap between the boards where they intersect so the finished box beam can be inserted over the 2" × 6" support board.

4. If joists are not present where a beam is being installed, hold up the 2" × 6" board and center on the chalk line. Nail it into place with a finish nailer to prevent it from shifting. Drill pilot holes in the desired locations at each end and in the center of the board, through the board and into the ceiling. Gently pull off the board and mark the pilot holes on the ceiling with a pencil (so they aren't confused with a nail hole). Remove the nails from the 2" × 6" board with pliers or wire clippers. Tap wall anchors into the pilot holes with a hammer, and screw them into place. Hold the board up to the ceiling again and

4.

4.

5.

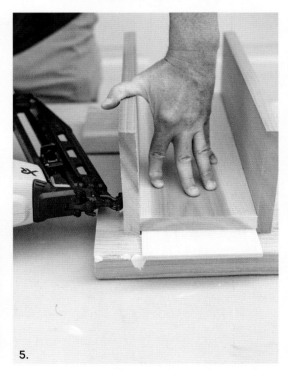

5.

line up the pilot holes with the anchors. Nail it into place. Insert the screws through the pilot holes and into the wall anchors.

5. Build U-shaped boxes to fit over the 2" × 6" support boards out of premium 1" × 6" boards. Cut the 1" × 6" boards to size by taping them tightly together with painter's tape and cutting them to size. This will ensure that all three pieces are exactly the same size. Dry fit one board on the ceiling to make sure the measurement is accurate. Make adjustments, if necessary, before assembling the beam.

6. Dry fit the boxes over the support beams to ensure a proper fit.

7. Prime and paint the box beams.

8. Install the beams by positioning them over the 2" × 6" support boards and nailing them into the 2" × 6" supports with a nailer. Reinforce with screws inserted through the beam into the 2" × 6" boards on each side. Use screws with small heads so they can be covered by crown molding or trim, or easily filled in with paintable wood filler.

9. Install trim or crown molding inside each "box" to hide the screws and nail holes. Caulk all visible seams and gaps in the beams. Caulk and paint the trim.

The Living Spaces for Your
Season of Life

There was a time when the living room of our Pennsylvania house looked more like a day care than a living room. There was a row of toys—bouncy seats, ExerSaucers, swings, Jumparoos. I loved and hated those toys! They kept my boys, who were born seventeen months apart, occupied and happy while I worked on other things, but the part of me that wanted everything to be pretty and coordinated struggled with the bright colors and bulky sizes. Not only did they not add anything to the decorating aesthetic, but they detracted from it!

My boys grew out of those toys years ago and they were passed along to sit in the middle of other living rooms, where they occupied and delighted other babies. The point is they were in my living room for only a short season and they will be in that next living room for only a short season. We have to be both accepting and realistic about the seasons of life and the physical needs that our home will meet along the way.

This is especially true in living spaces. We have a playroom in our current home with a TV and game system, a wall of Lego blocks and people organized by color, guitars, and a drum kit. I imagined it would be a little hideaway, a boy cave. They would disappear into the basement and wouldn't surface again until dinner. When they want to play with toys, though, guess what happens? They haul them out of the playroom and up the steps to the living room!

A good living space can be, and maybe should be, like a magnet. It's comfortable, it's right in the middle of the action, and it's where everyone wants to congregate. In a modern family where our schedules are full of activities and events, that's a good thing! It might involve setting aside a cabinet for games and toys, reserving a corner for a play kitchen, or even making room for a hospital bed. Be patient with the seasons that come with messes and gear. That's the entire point of living spaces, right? To *live* there. To allow life to fill the space in all of its messiness and imperfection and seasons.

kitchens

kitch·en

/ˈkiCH(ə)n/

noun

a room where food is kept, prepared, and cooked

THE MORE YOU KNOW, THE MORE YOU CAN CREATE.
THERE IS NO END TO IMAGINATION IN THE KITCHEN.
—*JULIA CHILD*

I bet that you can fill in the blank here. The _____ is the heart of the home.

If you said "kitchen," you're right *and* I was right. High fives all around. The kitchen is not only declared to be the heart of the home, but it's also said to be the room with the highest rate of return when it comes to renovation and resale value.

We were so good at that, let's try another one.

_____ and _____ sell houses.

I'm going to cheat and tell you the answer is not "location" and "location," which would be a terrible sentence, anyway. You were probably right again and said "kitchens" and "baths" sell houses. While this conventional realtor saying doesn't always play out in reality (someone bought the home I lived in through middle school because they loved the dogwood trees in the yard), the notion is rooted in what they see in the market as they help clients buy and sell homes.

I'm not a real estate expert, but as a home lover and a home-improvement junkie, I would guess that saying has something to do with kitchens and baths being expensive to renovate. Rooms that don't involve plumbing, electrical, appliances, and built-in fixtures are typically going to be much easier to update and customize than rooms that are filled with those things.

So, from a practical and financial perspective, we hit the house-hunting bull's-eye if we can find a home with a kitchen that fits our style down to the last detail. The tile is the right color, pattern, sheen, and material. Not only are the cabinets arranged to fit your belongings perfectly, but the finish is just what you would pick if you were designing a kitchen from scratch. The countertop is the thing that dreams are made of. Even the lighting is the ideal balance of task and ambient.

Beyond that, the heart of the home, the kitchen, already *feels* like the heart of the home to us. There is something familiar about it even if it's new.

But that is not what usually happens. In the typical house-hunting scenario, there is normally at least one thing that misses the mark when it comes to your tastes and preferences. You have to look past the dark and dated cabinetry or the fact that you can't have the dishwasher and the refrigerator open at the same time or the tiled backsplash with the classic 1990s Tuscan grape motif.

It's still the place where meals are prepared and the kids sit on the barstools for after-school snacks, but it doesn't feel like yours.

If compromises have to be made in the kitchen (and they most likely do), I want to offer up a glimmer of hope. Many issues with suburban kitchens (not all, but many) are strictly cosmetic, and with some elbow grease along with hiring out a few tasks that are beyond your DIY ability, you can completely transform your kitchen. It might not be the dream kitchen you would design from scratch, but it can be *your* kitchen, one that looks and feels like you and one that is worthy of being the heart that beats for the family who lives there.

Assignment:
CREATING YOUR DREAM KITCHEN

Gather a collection of images of kitchens that you love (virtually or physically in a folder or on a pin board). What do those kitchens have in common with one another? What do they have in common with your kitchen? What are changes that can be easily made in your kitchen to emulate those you love? Is there anything you can do today, like clearing the clutter and rearranging the accessories? What are the midrange projects that require some planning but can be completed without great expense? Are there big projects you can start planning and saving for?

Our Typical Suburban Kitchen

I have to admit that I was excited about our kitchen when I first saw it in the real estate listing. I could tell that it had good bones and it wouldn't take much to customize it to suit my design aesthetic. This was pretty important to me, because I was moving away from a wonderful kitchen that we had customized with painted cabinetry (there were over fifty doors that I hand painted), a built-in range hood, and butcher-block counters that we fabricated, finished, and installed ourselves. I had ample storage and I loved that kitchen. It was going to be hard to beat.

I liked this kitchen right off the bat, though, and I had a good feeling about it. It was like meeting someone who you know will be a good friend. It's just going to work. I knew a lot of paint would be involved and a few other cosmetic changes, but a huge kitchen renovation that required doing dishes in the bathtub for a few months wasn't going to be in our future. I could see that small and simple changes, like swapping out the modern pendant lights over the island for recessed lights and hanging my pot rack over the island, would contribute to the look I wanted at a low cost.

Both the fridge and the dishwasher needed to be replaced immediately (the freezer wall was cracked, the dishwasher was on its last leg after working for thirteen years without a water softener), and I have never been a fan of electric ranges, so we budgeted to replace all of the appliances right when we moved in. During the initial phase of the kitchen makeover, the dual-fuel

range (along with running a gas line to it) was the big splurge. We made the rest of the changes ourselves—painting the cabinetry, swapping out the modern brushed nickel hardware for glass pulls, changing out the light fixtures, and hanging the pot rack. Those simple and comparatively inexpensive changes completely transformed the look of the kitchen.

We could've stopped there, but a year later, we swapped the dark granite counters for a lighter, brighter quartz and had a marble subway tile backsplash installed. With the addition of the almost-white counters, I painted the island in a custom-mixed rich green to set it apart from the other cabinets and make it a little more interesting. White on white on white can be lovely, but it was looking a little stark in my kitchen. The green island added just the right amount of color.

While some of the big changes, like putting in the beefy range and my dream countertops, made a bigger splash, it was the simple process of painting the cabinetry, the largest surface area in the kitchen, that made the greatest impact.

Customizing
Cabinetry

Since the cabinets take up the most physical and visual space in a typical kitchen and it really is the best way to make an update or change on a budget, this chapter is going to focus primarily on customizing them. Before we get into painting cabinets, let's talk about customizing typical, ho-hum cabinets. It is amazing how adding a few custom details can make builder-grade cabinets look high-end.

groove boards, wallpaper, tile, a bold paint color, or a custom-cut mirror in the back of the open cabinet!

REMOVING CABINET DOORS

This is one of my favorite options for customizing kitchen cabinets, because it's free! You don't have to go out and buy something new. It's just removing something that is already there. The downside to removing cabinet doors is that you lose the closed storage, but the advantage is that the room is visually opened up. If you have beautiful dishes, glasses, and cookware, this is a great way to put those pieces on display.

To add another layer of visual interest or texture, consider adding beadboard, tongue-and-

ADDING CORBELS

Corbels are an easy and relatively inexpensive way to customize upper cabinets or overhanging counters. New corbels can be painted to match the cabinets so they look like they were always there. Antique corbels can add a sense of eclecticism and history, even to newer homes. Both options add architectural interest to a kitchen.

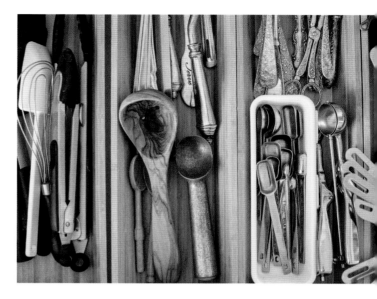

REPLACING HARDWARE

Replacing the hardware on a piece of furniture is a simple and inexpensive way to change the look of a dated piece. The same principle is true in the kitchen, but the cost can easily reach into the hundreds of dollars when hardware is being purchased for twenty cabinet doors and drawers! Just keep this in mind when budgeting your makeover. It seems like a cheap change, but all of those handles and knobs can add up!

That being said, changing out the hardware is still an excellent way to update and customize cabinets.

CUSTOMIZING THE INTERIORS

This doesn't sound as exciting as adding corbels or changing outdated hardware, but the first time you use that pullout trash drawer, you might think otherwise! Customize the interiors of cabinets with sliding shelves, dividers, baskets, and organizing trays. Yes, this makes the kitchen more functional, but it also makes it a more enjoyable space to cook and prepare meals.

ADDING TRIM

Adding trim is especially effective if the existing cabinetry lacks any sort of detail, inset panels, crown molding, routed edges, etc. Tacking on some trim to create the illusion of panels or to visually extend the height of short upper cabinets can elevate even the simplest cabinet designs.

Project: PAINTING CABINETRY

Bloggers, home magazines, TV shows, hardware stores, and paint companies have been beating this drum for years, but there is good reason for that, and I'm going to beat it as well. The best and cheapest way to completely transform and update any kitchen is to paint the cabinets.

Everything else in the kitchen can be wrong, but as soon as you paint those dated, dark, tired cabinets, the kitchen will immediately look different. There still might be bigger fish to fry, like changing the counters or tiling a backsplash or replacing mismatched appliances, but a fresh coat of paint will get the kitchen moving in the right direction. A direction toward having a customized kitchen that you love.

As an enthusiast of any kind of paint as well as the miracle it can be when it comes to transforming just about anything, I've found that painting kitchen cabinets was a no-brainer update in all three homes we owned.

In my first home, the cabinet priming and painting started hours after closing. In my second home, I was pregnant and then caring for a newborn and then another newborn seventeen months later, so it took me a few years to tackle that kitchen. In our most recent home, I started painting the cabinets within a month. And each time, painting the cabinets a bright, clean white made the house immediately feel more like home.

While I love white cabinetry for the classic and neutral backdrop it provides, there isn't a wrong color to paint cabinetry. It can be colorful and bold, dark and moody, or bright and cheerful. It just has to be you.

Having painted several kitchens myself, I know that painting cabinets is hard work and it can be daunting, especially if you haven't done it before. Don't worry, though. I'm going to give you all of the details to do it from start to finish. And I assure you that this is an ideal project even for novice DIYers.

SELECTING THE RIGHT COLOR FOR YOUR CABINETS

As I said, there isn't a right or wrong color, but certain colors are going to look more traditional, more modern, or more eclectic. Since painting kitchen cabinets is a big job, I would suggest choosing a color that you know you can live with for a long time. It's okay if that color is strong or bold or if it's neutral and quiet. Just pick something that feels classic and timeless to you, that will also work with your counter, backsplash tile, flooring, etc.

White, black, gray, and putty or greige colors are all popular and timeless choices, but there is a wide range of options just in that limited color pool! It's always a good idea to purchase a few samples and to paint swatches onto sample boards (which can be purchased in the paint department at most hardware or paint stores). Tape these large swatches up onto the cabinets and watch them as the light in your house changes.

To throw another wrinkle in the decision-making process, the cabinets don't all have to be painted one color. An island is a great place to add a pop of an accent color to turn it into your statement piece. Base cabinets can be a different color than the upper cabinets in order to set them apart and break up the monotony of row upon row of cabinet doors. Stand-alone pantries are another great place to add some color contrast and something unexpected.

WHAT YOU'LL NEED

- 150-grit sandpaper (A palm sander will really speed things along.)
- Grease-cutting soap or cleaner (like TSP)
- Quality primer (I like Zinsser Smart Prime.)
- Quality water-based enamel paint in a satin or semigloss finish (Check out pages 220–229 for information on a variety of paint options to pick what's best for your project.)
- Paint roller
- 6" microfiber roller covers
- Paint tray and liners
- 2" synthetic angled sash brush

A FEW HELPFUL TIPS

- Always test the products first. Test out the prepping, primer, and paint on the side of one cabinet or on one door first. Do that entire section from start to finish in order to practice and make sure you're getting the desired look. (It's better to make mistakes on a small section than on your entire kitchen!)
- Take the time to prep! I know it's not glamorous and you just want to get right to the fun part of the transformation, but quality prep work is the key to a beautiful finish.
- Use quality products. Using good applicators and quality primer and paint will make a huge difference in the end result. When it comes to home improvement, there are many good places to exercise thriftiness, but paint isn't one of those places.
- Work one section at a time. Painting cabinets is a straightforward, simple project, but that doesn't mean it's easy. It is hard work, and you're working in a very busy room in the house. Do yourself a favor and work on it in small, manageable chunks. It'll spread the project out over a few days or weeks, which might be against your nature, but it'll reduce stress and mitigate the temptation to get sloppy as the finish line is in sight.

1. REMOVE THE DOORS. Believe it or not, when I painted those first cabinets in my town house, I did it with the doors on! I just cut around the hinges and squeezed my brush tip into tight corners. It is so, so much easier to just remove the doors. First off, the doors can be sprayed, if you have that capability, but also the paint will self-level if the door is lying flat, and it's easier to paint the cabinets themselves without the doors and hinges in the way. (If the hinges are hidden, i.e., not visible when closed, leave them on the cabinets. They have been adjusted so the door hangs level, and removing them will cause a lot more work for you! They are easy to paint around. Also, number the doors and the cabinets with painter's tape so you can easily match them up when it's time to hang them.)

2. CLEAN THE CABINETS. It doesn't matter how neat and tidy your kitchen is, if anyone has ever cooked in your kitchen, there will be a nice, thin layer of airborne grease stuck on your cabinets. You don't see it or notice it as you work in your kitchen every day, but it's there, and paint does not like to stick to it. Take some time to clean it off with a grease-cutting soap or cleaner. Scrub each cabinet door and cabinet well and dry them with old towels. Make sure the cabinets are completely dry before moving on to the next step.

3. SAND. This step isn't about stripping the finish off the cabinets but about roughing up the surface to allow the primer to get a better grip on the slick surface. I typically use an 80- to 150-grit sanding pad on an orbital palm sander for sanding cabinets and furniture. The lower the sandpaper number, the rougher the grit. If your cabinets are really glossy or you're sanding by hand, opt for 80 grit. If the finish is mostly worn away or you're using a mechanized sander, 100–150 will do the trick. Wipe off the dust with a damp cloth or tack cloth. Always wear a dust mask when sanding. (You will have bits of your cabinet inside your nose if you don't. Don't say I didn't warn you!)

4. PRIME. So, now let's talk about priming. Using a quality primer is every bit as important as using a quality paint. It may be even more important, because it is the foundation that will help the paint grip the prefinished surface of the cabinets. I use a quality brush (a 2" angled sash is my favorite) for the trim and small parts of the faces of the cabinets. Work in long, smooth strokes and continue to review the paint you've applied to check for drips. For the larger areas, like the cabinet sides, use a microfiber roller to minimize roller marks. Generously load the roller with paint but roll slowly to prevent splatters. Roll in a narrow W shape to distribute the paint over the cabinet. Once the paint is applied in an even coat, roll back over it without reloading the roller with paint. Use light pressure. This is just to smooth out the primer and knock down any edges caused by the roller.

And I'll throw out a warning so you're not alarmed. Primer always looks ugly. It looks messy, you can see brushstrokes and roller marks, but it's okay. What matters, at this point, is how it *feels*, not how it looks. And I'm not referring to how it feels in your heart and soul. I mean how it feels to the touch. It should feel smooth, even if it doesn't look it.

If necessary, sand your primed piece with 220-grit paper after the primer dries. This is just to smooth out any drips that might have happened or any texture left from the roller. I know you'll be antsy to move on to the next step, but it's

3.

4.

best to allow the primer to cure for two to three days prior to painting. It helps with overall adhesion, which is important for kitchen cabinets that are constantly being opened and closed.

5. PAINT. For painting cabinetry, I love using a waterborne enamel in a satin finish. It's a water-based paint with a hard finish that behaves a bit more like an oil but is easier to clean up and not as stinky. It has a long open time, which means you can brush over it, fix drips, etc. without pulling off the drying paint. I think the reason I like using this paint so much, though, is that it has a relatively thin consistency. The advantage of thinner paint is that it's self-leveling. Brush and roller marks disappear, making for a beautiful finish. The disadvantage is it doesn't cover quite as well as a thicker paint, which means more coats, and you do have to keep an eye out for drips.

Apply the paint in the same manner as the primer was applied. Typically, two coats will be required for full coverage.

Now, I know you might be wondering about a topcoat. If you use a quality paint with a satin gloss (or glossier), you do not need to apply a topcoat. It is basically built into the paint. It will dry hard and will be durable and wipeable.

Most paints and finishes take thirty days to fully cure. You can put the doors back on when they are dry to the touch, but just ask your family to be gentle with them during that cure time.

Jeff laughed when I requested that of him and asked, "How exactly do I do that?"

"I don't know! *Just be gentle with them!*"

APPLYING PAINT WITH A SPRAYER

If you have a lot of cabinetry to paint, you might want to consider purchasing or renting a paint sprayer. If you want to go that route, here are some tips about purchasing or renting a sprayer and using one:

- When looking to rent or purchase a sprayer, look for one that holds the paint in a small cup attached to the sprayer as opposed to a larger reservoir that feeds the paint to the sprayer through a hose. Those are a real challenge to clean and some will hold almost a quart of paint in the hose!
- USE A SPRAY TENT. Overspray is a real thing, and you will make a mess if you try to spray in a garage or basement. Set up a spray tent outside and use plenty of drop cloths to cover the surrounding areas.
- DON'T SPRAY ON A WINDY DAY. This might be obvious, but I've been impatient enough to try it, and it was a ridiculous decision! The overspray was blowing all over the place and my tent kept taking flight.
- DRESS HEAD TO TOE FOR SPRAYING. The overspray could possibly get on your shoes, your clothes, in your hair, etc., so wear old clothes and old shoes.
- WEAR A RESPIRATOR MASK. This needs to be an actual respirator mask, not just a dust mask. A dust mask just isn't going to catch all of the fine paint spray, and it's very important to protect your lungs.
- PRACTICE FIRST. Practice with the sprayer by just running water through it and spraying it on a piece of cardboard. This will help you get used to the way the sprayer works. When you're doing well with that, start spraying primer, but still practice on a piece of cardboard until your sprayed paint looks smooth and even. There shouldn't be drips (too thin) or splatters (too thick).
- THIN THE PRIMER OR PAINT. Add water to thin the primer or paint so it goes through the sprayer without splattering. I like to mix my paint until it's thin enough to run off a stir stick in a steady string. (Most paint runs off in a ribbon, which is too thick for a sprayer.)
- START SPRAYING IN THE AIR. Pull the trigger on the spray gun when it's not pointed at what you're painting. Splatters and drips are most likely to happen right when the paint starts coming out of the nozzle. These drips will just fall on your drop cloth instead of on your cabinet door. So start spraying and then move the spray gun over the cabinet in smooth, even strokes until the door is covered in a thin, even coat.
- KEEP THE SPRAY GUN MOVING. Don't leave the spray gun pointed in one spot for too long or it will cause the paint to have an "orange-peel" texture. Also, rotate the thing you're painting so you spray it from all angles.

Assignment: PRACTICE PAINTING

If you want to paint your kitchen cabinets but you are new to painting, buy a cheap piece of furniture from a thrift store or yard sale (or pick one up for free from a local recycling center, free classifieds, or the curb) and use it for practice. Test out brushes, rollers, paint, and paint colors without any pressure. When it comes time to paint your cabinets, you'll be so glad you have that experience under your belt!

The *Customization* Miracle Worker

I talk a lot about paint in this book and in this chapter because it is without question the number one, biggest-bang-for-the-buck way to customize your home and most of the things in it. It can give you a clean slate, set a mood, add a pop of color, and completely transform the entire look and feel of a room. Paint is your friend no matter your budget, but it is especially helpful when you're trying to decorate on a dime.

And the best part? You can paint just about anything.

CAN I PAINT...
LAMINATE CABINETS?

Yes! I painted the laminate cabinets in my laundry room, and they have held up very well. Paint is a wonderful way to elevate laminate cabinets, which are sturdy, but can look cheap and clinical.

The key is to use a quality adhesion primer that is made for slick, nonporous surfaces and to give it time to cure before heavy use.

TILE?

Absolutely! As with laminate cabinets, the key is to use a good adhesion primer made for difficult surfaces like tile. I would also suggest sanding the tile prior to painting it. That might seem like an odd step, but the abrasions created by sanding will give the surface tooth that the paint can grip. Cure time is also important to reduce

dings and scratches, so wait thirty days before dragging things along the floor or allowing water to sit.

COUNTERS?

Again, yes! And there are even some amazing kits out there to emulate marble or granite with paint. It's an inexpensive way to update outdated or worn countertops until it's in the budget to replace them. Prep work (sanding and cleaning) and using a high-quality primer are the keys to longevity. Also, use a paint that can handle wet environments, since it's likely to have water sitting on it at some point. To extend the life of the paint, wipe off water and spills as soon as possible and always use a cutting board.

APPLIANCES?

How else can I say yes? Affirmative! Yes, you can paint appliances and can actually have a lot of fun with them. I've seen fridges painted as chalkboards or bright colors to make a design statement. Just use a primer that will adhere to slick surfaces along with a quality paint and apply it with a roller for smooth surfaces. If you're painting a stove or oven, make sure you use a paint that is intended for high heat.

The Kitchen
Overhaul

Some kitchens have good bones, so paint and cosmetic changes are all that is required to customize them. There are times, though, when the existing layout just isn't going to work. If you're going to totally gut and overhaul a room, even a relatively new and nice one, a kitchen is a great candidate and one that is worth the investment. Renovating a kitchen typically improves the value and salability of the home, and it's a room that is used multiple times every day. If renovating isn't worth it from a real estate perspective, it's worth it for the enjoyment of you and your family.

Cheri Dietzman of Rochester, Minnesota, and Michael Wurm Jr. of Pittsburgh both completely renovated their kitchens. (See before pictures of these spaces on page 287.) Michael's home, built in 1955, had a small and dated kitchen that was last renovated in the 1990s. In addition to loving to cook, Michael creates, tests, photographs, and shares recipes online and for magazines. The kitchen was the ideal place to start when it came to making this house feel like his home.

Michael has experience with decorating and interior design, but this was his first major renovation, so he collaborated on the remodel with a local designer, Katy Popple. She helped with details such as building codes, space planning, functional layout, lighting, and plumbing. Michael was also able to consult with her on color selections and finishes in order to bring his vision to life. About the kitchen makeover, Michael shared, "Since I started from the ground up, I was able to choose features and design elements that suited my lifestyle and made me smile: a brass faucet, butler's pantry with beautiful open shelving, built-in coffeemaker, and so many other details. The kitchen instantly became an inviting space in my home."

The kitchen in Cheri's 1978 split-level home featured knotty pine cabinets, linoleum floors and dark paneling, and had a cramped layout. Cheri and her handy husband, Kirk, gutted the kitchen, replaced the linoleum and Berber carpeting with hardwood floors, reconfigured the kitchen to include an island and make the layout more functional, and replaced the cabinetry and lighting. They kept the paneling and simply painted it to lighten and brighten the space while retaining the charming cottage feel. In addition, they scraped the popcorn texture off the ceiling in order to update the space and keep the attention on the wood beams.

The Dietzmans hired skilled tradesmen when needed, but they did the majority of the work themselves in order to stay within budget.

This is how Cheri replied when I asked what feels like home to her: "To me, home is a meaningful, fresh, comfortable place where loved ones gather, meaningful connections are celebrated, and lasting memories are made. A place my family longs to return to and be."

The *Everyday* on Display

One of the trickiest things about decorating a kitchen is that it is a utilitarian space, and there are a lot of well-used items in the kitchen that aren't exactly pretty to look at. There's the bulky microwave, the space-age blender, and the bright yellow plastic dish brush. Kitchens are magnets for things that are useful, but not beautiful, and most of it is on display whether we intentionally choose it or not. If it sits out all the time (from the pile of mail by the front door to the coffeemaker on the counter), it's on display.

I have a vintage bike basket filled with toilet paper rolls in our half bathroom (see page 202), and when I shared it on my blog, one of my readers said she wouldn't want to use toilet paper as decor. The comment made me smile. I didn't consider it decor in that I wouldn't hang it over our fireplace in the living room, but I viewed it as a way to make something that needed to be accessible a little prettier.

Your coffeemaker or faucet or bagel slicer might not be considered decor, but if they are sitting out all the time, I hate to break it to you, they sort of are. They are collectively a part of your "look."

This is compounded in most kitchens by the fact that counter space is at a premium. I rarely hear people complain about having an overabundance of counter space. In most kitchens, every square inch of counter space has to be claimed and protected, defended regularly against mail, backpacks, school projects, abandoned drinking glasses, and the latest fad appliance. So, the appliances, knife blocks, utensil holders, cutting boards, and fruit bowls are the decor of the kitchen.

Being particular about aesthetics, I decided I would try to find a new home for our black toaster oven, which looked like a black hole in our mostly white kitchen. I opened every cabinet to see if it would possibly work in one. *Maybe we could keep it on a shelf with sliders and pull it out and plug it in when we needed to use it, or maybe we could put it in the pantry with the microwave or on the wet bar counter in the basement?* I tried every scenario just to get that toaster off the counter. In the end, none of the options would really work. They all looked better than having the toaster sitting on the counter, but would make actually *using it*, which we did almost every day, an annoying process. Not to mention that having a toaster oven inside a cabinet could possibly be a fire hazard.

Jeff walked into the room as I was balancing the bulky toaster on my knees, trying to fit it into a bottom cabinet. I knew he wouldn't approve, and I was totally busted. His face said it all. *There is no way in the world that toaster is going into the cabinet. You might as well surrender and put it back.*

In the end, I waited until the toaster's life was almost over and replaced it with one that I wouldn't mind having on display. If it's going to be out, visible, and part of the decor, take the time

to buy something you like. You don't need to go on a crusade to do it all at once, but gradually over time, as needed, replace things you don't like with things you do.

Over the years, I've slowly traded plastic spoons and spatulas for wooden ones, plastic dish brushes for those with wood handles and natural bristles, sponges for crocheted dishcloths, cotton dish towels for linen. I look for fun saltshakers and for cookbooks that not only contain tasty recipes, but also look pretty sitting on a shelf. Every decision keeps form and function in mind: *Will I use it? Do I love it? Does it reinforce my idea of home or detract from it?*

I admit that it's an overly romantic way to shop for basic household items, but why not? When you can enjoy a vintage orange juicer that reminds you of the one your great-grandma used instead of one that's strictly functional, why not? Be picky in the little, everyday objects. Every choice, even the ones that are made out of necessity, is a chance to customize your home and its contents.

Assignment:
MAKE A SWAP

Replace one utilitarian item that isn't attractive with one you find beautiful. Maybe it's something you already own and you can discover a new, everyday use for it.

CHAPTER V

DINING *spaces*

din·ing
/'dīniNG/
noun
the activity of eating a meal

AS WE EVOLVE, OUR HOMES SHOULD AS WELL.
—SUZANNE TUCKER INTERIORS

The Dining Room Doesn't Have to Be a *Dining Room*

The first time in my adult life that I had a formal dining room in a home I owned was when we moved into our 1948 Cape Cod in a two-stoplight town in Pennsylvania. Until the day we closed on that house, I'd had only breakfast nooks and eat-in kitchens. Owning a formal dining room marks the transition into full-blown adulthood. So, of course, I needed to populate it with a table, chairs, and a buffet. I already had a lovely antique buffet handed down to me by my parents and, after we spent a few tableless months, someone passed a displaced dining set along to us.

The sturdy and basic set of table and chairs was the first of about eight different sets to occupy that room. It became somewhat of a joke that our dining room furniture was perpetually for sale, sold, and replaced. The main driving force behind that was I bought, refinished, and sold furniture as a part of my business and I wasn't one to turn away a good offer, even if the piece was in my home. But, at the heart of that rotation was the fact that we really didn't sit and eat at that table. We didn't dine in our dining room, so I didn't feel protective of the furniture we used for that space. There weren't sentimental attachments, and a gaping hole in the center of the room wasn't the kind of disruption we'd experience if our sofa were missing.

We ate a few meals in there for holidays or when we had guests, but that was only a handful of times each year. Most of the time, we congregated at the kitchen table, outside on the deck, or in the soft seating of the family room.

Our dining room was used a lot, though. It had the best light in the house, so it became my favorite place to take photographs for my blog. It was a storage room when I was getting ready for shows. The large work surface became a makeshift sewing desk when I worked on projects and a packing table when we were shipping online orders. The dining room might've been one of the rooms in the house that was used most often outside of the kitchen, but rarely for its intended purpose.

I think this is a pretty common scenario and, if you have a home that was built in recent years, the square footage generally reserved for a dining room may have even been designated as an office or merged into a larger great room. If you do have a dining room, as I do currently, it doesn't have to be used as one.

Your house should serve *you*. You shouldn't feel obligated to use one room in a particular way just because it is labeled as such on the real estate listing. I think we often do, without really considering other options. *Well, it's opposite the living room and off the kitchen, therefore I have to fill it with a table, chairs, and a matching buffet, topped off with a chandelier.*

If you use a dining room, and if it serves you

as a dining room, then by all means, use it as a dining room. If it's a room that is more often used for school projects, card games, and business ventures, or it isn't used at all, then maybe it's time to claim that room for another purpose One of the easiest ways to customize a home is by changing the function and purpose of a room simply by making different furniture choices.

Here are just a few suggestions:

- Studio
- Office
- Sitting room
- Playroom
- Craft/sewing room
- Library
- Music room
- Schoolroom

If you are using your dining room in a non-traditional way, I would suggest getting some ideas from the chapters on living spaces (see chapter III) and creative and work spaces (see chapter VII).

Shaunna Parker started using her dining room as a studio and creative space so she could squeeze some painting and work in while being accessible to her kids. "I've found that once I bit the bullet and threw traditional out the window, I create something in that room almost every day, even if just for a few minutes. I'm in love with it and will probably never go back to a formal dining room again!"

Shaunna Parker set up her studio in the formal dining room to make better use of the space and to paint and create while still spending time with her family.

HOME TO ME IS REST.
SPACES THAT MAKE ME FEEL LIKE I AM
HONORING THE THINGS I LOVE,
THE BEAUTY THAT SPEAKS TO ME,
AND HONOR HOW OUR FAMILY USES THE
SPACE...THAT'S HOME. HOME IS MY PEOPLE.
I WILL ALWAYS CONTINUE TO CREATE
SPACES THAT SERVE US FOR ALL OF WHO
WE ARE, NO MATTER WHERE THAT MAY BE.

—SHAUNNA PARKER

The Welcoming, *Traditional* Dining Room

When we first moved to Pennsylvania, we noticed an odd architectural trend on some of the old homes—there were two front doors. They were side by side, only about five or six feet apart. "What is the point of that?" I finally asked one of our friends who lived in a Civil War–era home that had two front doors. One door was to use every day, and one was for special occasions! One typically led into an informal room or hall used daily by the family, while the other led into a room reserved for weddings, funerals, and births.

Assignment:
DINING ROOM ASSESSMENT

It's time to assess your dining room! How many times a year do you use it? Do you ever wish you had one more room in your house for a specific purpose? Could your dining room meet that need? Would you miss not having a formal dining room? Ask the members of your family for their opinion on the dining room and how they would like to use it. You may discover some square footage that can be used in a more productive way or learn that your dining room is an important part of your lives and it's worth keeping as is.

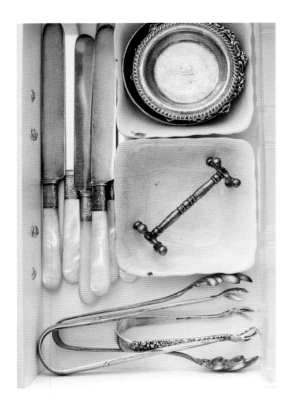

I bring this up because the idea of having a door or a room that is reserved strictly for specific life-altering events is so foreign to us in our current culture. I think without knowing it, though, we can do that to our dining rooms. They can *feel* reserved, off-limits, and like they are too precious to use.

I used to feel that way about dining rooms, fancy china, and linen napkins. I kept beautiful silver flatware that I inherited from my mom, grandmother, two great-grandmothers, and a great-great-grandmother in a silver chest 363 days of each year for a long time. I pulled them out for Christmas and Thanksgiving, because I had this idea that they were too expensive and delicate to use daily. I finally wondered why I wasn't using

these exquisite pieces that I loved every day. *Will one get mangled in the garbage disposal? Might one of the kids throw a fork away accidentally while clearing their plate?* I decided the answer to the questions was probably yes.

Since I couldn't make up my mind about using them every day and the damage or loss that might result from that decision, I asked my mom her opinion. I loved her answer. She informed me that my great-grandmother Rosa used them as her everyday flatware, so I certainly could, too.

Rosa passed away when I was about nine or ten, so I remember her, but I never really *knew* her. I always enjoyed stories about her, though. Her homemade congealed citrus salad (classic 1950s) is a staple at family holiday meals, but she used to make

This boxy, boring dining room was transformed into a customized space with the addition of a budget-friendly, hand-painted landscape mural.

it weekly, keeping single servings in little aluminum molds for her grandkids' visits. She mowed her own lawn into her seventies until she was run over by a rolling car that she tried to stop from going into the street where it might've hurt someone. She crocheted the most beautiful, intricate things without even looking. Her hands just knew what they were doing. She was a cool lady.

Using them would honor her, carrying on her tradition of using beautiful, fancy things on just a normal day of the week. I got them out of the silver chest and into the kitchen drawer that day.

We now use fine silver every single day and have for years. Some pieces date back to the 1800s and are engraved with initials and dates that tell a tiny piece of my family's story, including Rosa's. Yes, a couple of pieces have been victims of the disposal, and my boys have no idea that the knife they are using to bang on the rim of a jar lid that's stuck is over one hundred years old. It is just our silverware. We use it and that makes me happy.

A dining room is about gathering, about friends and family, about celebrating. And those are things that shouldn't be stuffy, sterile, or roped off. The furniture and pieces we use should be warm, welcoming, and approachable, even if it is more formal and traditional. If you decide to go in that direction, just remember that traditional doesn't mean boring, predictable, or something that has to be taken too seriously. Just like every other room in your home, you should love it and it should invite people to go inside, not to feel like they need to whisper and tiptoe so they don't break anything.

Despite the fact that my dining room is more of a multipurpose room, I chose to furnish it as a formal dining room for a few reasons.

ONE

I love tableware, table linens, flatware, and anything that's used for cooking, eating, and entertaining. When I was packing for our move from Pennsylvania to Minnesota, I decided to count all of the ironstone plates I had in my collection—146. And that was only the *dinner plates*.

It didn't seem like a lot of plates when they were just sitting in my cabinet, but when I faced packing them, it seemed a little crazy. I shared that number with Jeff and he smiled like he knew this all along. "You *do* know that our dining table only sits six people at a time." He quickly added, "And the solution is *not* to get a table that seats one hundred forty-six!"

What I love, though, is that Jeff didn't press me to get rid of any. He knew I was already parting with a lot of things in that one-thousand-mile move. And getting between me and ironstone, which is my favorite thing to collect, is not wise. As I was packing those 146 plates, though, I wondered why I don't collect something that is lightweight and not breakable! We used a lot of Bubble Wrap!

TWO

I often style and photograph tutorials and ideas for decorating and entertaining, so my dining room is photographed pretty regularly for my work. It's not conventional, but it's still serving me.

While this scenario isn't relatable for most people, you might have a similar reason for wanting a dining room—it's where you display your family china, you love setting a fancy table when you have friends over for tea, or it's the best room to work on puzzles.

THREE

I tend to be more traditional in my decorating style, so I like using the dining room in a traditional way. And, in my opinion, dining rooms can be a lot of fun to decorate!

The dining room in our current home was a bit of a challenge, though. It's more of a square than a rectangle, which is tricky when trying to fit a table with six chairs. It's also small and faces south, with the only window under the porch roof, so it's the darkest room in the house.

The first thing we did was replace the carpet with hardwood floors. This immediately made the space look more dining room–ish. After that step, I needed to think of a way to add some visual oomph. I had considered a wall of built-ins to showcase my ironstone collection, but ultimately, I decided on a wall mural.

Project: PAINTED WALL MURAL

I started painting this wall mural on a whim. I was literally in my pajamas and hadn't even eaten breakfast. My boys were probably raised by wolves that morning. But I had this idea that I had been thinking about, dreaming about, wondering about for a while. *Can I pull it off? Will it look good?* It was time to end the suspense and just put the paint on the wall and satisfy those questions.

It turned out better than I imagined, and it was easier and quicker than I thought it would be. DIY projects tend to be the opposite—harder, longer, and more expensive than planned—but this one defied the norm. It was "free," because I had everything on hand, and I was able to complete the dramatic makeover in just a few hours over a couple of days.

If the idea of painting a wall mural yourself sounds about as possible as traversing Antarctica or going over Niagara Falls in a barrel, this mural isn't like other murals. It's loose, drippy, and imperfect, and it looks better that way. While it does require paint and a brush, it doesn't require the renderer to be a self-proclaimed artist sporting a beret and smock. It just requires a willingness to try.

WHAT YOU'LL NEED

- Neutral, creamy white base color (I used Pearly White by Sherwin-Williams in a matte finish.)
- Milk paint in a variety of greens and pale blues (I used Miss Mustard Seed's Milk Paint in Lucketts Green, Boxwood, Linen, Shutter Gray, and Kitchen Scale. You need only a very little amount of paint since you will water it down so much. Sample sizes in these colors will complete an entire room.)
- Water
- Plastic cups for mixing paint
- Paint stir sticks (or plastic spoons)
- Acrylic craft paint in burnt umber
- 2½" angled sash brush
- 3" chip brush

- Paint roller
- ⅜"-nap roller cover
- Paint tray
- Painter's tape (optional)
- Drop cloth
- Stepladder
- Chalk
- Artist brushes in wedge and filbert shapes
- Clear protective coat

A FEW HELPFUL TIPS

- Relax! It's just paint and you can always wash it off or paint over it if you don't like it. Practice first on a wall you are planning to paint anyway so there is no pressure. You can also practice on a sample board.
- Make sure your colors are very watery and soft. It's amazing how much a tiny bit of color can show up when it's brushed all over the wall. You'll notice through the tutorial that I use the same base color

(Lucketts Green) for all of the elements. The color is just adjusted slightly, creating a sense of harmony. This mural will run away from you and look harsh if your colors are too strong.

- Step back every ten to fifteen minutes to take in the overall look of the mural. When you look at one of the trees close up, it's sort of a mess of leaves and drips, but when you step back, it has a great effect!

- Be intentional about it not being perfect. The leaves, grass—everything will look better if they are random and not overthought. Put on some good music and allow yourself to get into a groove. If you find yourself getting tight, just walk away for a while.

- Remember that your "hand" is different from mine. Trying to copy my mural exactly is like trying to copy my signature or my handwriting. Yours will look different and that's a good thing! Embrace the uniqueness of your mural created by your hand.

- Don't judge the mural until it's done, and know that there will always be parts of it that "bother" you. There are a few clumps of grass that I wish I had done a little differently, but done is better than perfect!

STEPS

1. PAINT THE BASE WALL COLOR. Just paint this as you would a normal room! I suggest using a quality paint with a matte finish. Apply the paint with a ⅜"-nap roller, cutting in with a 2½" angled sash brush. Tape off the trim with painter's tape, if desired. Allow the base coat to dry completely.

2. PICK A "HORIZON LINE" TO DIVIDE THE LAND AND THE SKY. This shouldn't be exactly at the halfway point between the ceiling and the floor, but either above or below that center line. (For some reason, that just looks better to the eye!) Make a light pencil mark along that line. It doesn't have to be perfectly straight, but you don't want any extreme angles.

3. PAINT THE LAND. (I used Lucketts Green for the land and needed only about two tablespoons of powdered milk paint mix with about a cup of water, so the mixture was very thin.) Brush the land color on with a 3" chip brush using horizontal strokes. The color should get slightly lighter or more transparent toward the horizon line and darker toward the floor. Allow the paint to be a little drippy in a few places so it will give some interesting texture. Remember, this is just the foundation, so there will be trees and tufts of grass over it.

4. PAINT THE SKY. (I used a mixture of Linen, Shutter Gray, and Lucketts Green to make a soft blue-green-gray sky.) Use the chip brush to apply water to a small section of the wall above the horizon line. Dip the same brush into just a little bit of the sky color and brush it onto the wet section of the wall. The pigment will flow and drip through the water, creating a beautiful, barely-there effect. The color should be a little stronger toward and along the ceiling (or crown molding) and get more translucent as it heads down the wall, giving a sense of depth and clouds.

5. PAINT DISTANT HILLS. Using a mix slightly bluer than the land color (I used Kitchen Scale mixed with Lucketts Green), paint some loose, distant hills along the horizon line.

6. ADD DISTANT TREES. In the example of my mural, I added evergreens because of their simple shape. This color should be slightly darker than the color used for the distant hills. (I just added more Kitchen Scale to the same mix.) The distant trees should sit in front of the mountains or hills, not on top of them. You can also emphasize land around them, just to give them something to sit on.

7. ADD FOREGROUND TREES. For the trees in the foreground, start out by drawing a trunk and branches with chalk, just to ensure you like the shape and placement before adding paint. Changes can be made by simply wiping the chalk away with a damp paper towel and starting again. With a watered-down version of a light green (I used Lucketts Green again), brush on random "clumps" to create the overall shape of the tree and the beginning of bunches of leaves. Add layers of leaves in a darker green (I used Boxwood with some Lucketts Green mixed in)

using a filbert artist brush. Work in layers, one over the other, with the paint a little darker on some leaves and lighter on others to create variation. This technique gives the tree a bit more depth, even though it is a very two-dimensional folk art tree. Paint the trunk in a pale green (I used Linen and Lucketts Green) mixed with a tiny bit of burnt umber artist's acrylic paint. This makes a nice, soft brown.

8. ADD GRASSES AND BRUSH. Last, use an artist brush (I used a wedge brush here) to add some clusters of grass and brush in a darker green. (I used Boxwood.) If a stronger color is desired for these foreground elements, use acrylic paints that are more saturated in color. As with the trees, add these elements in layers to create depth, with more translucent grasses applied first.

9. If desired, add a protective topcoat once the mural is completely finished and dry.

Dressing Up or Dressing Down
a Dining Room

Sometimes the architecture of the home is going to dictate how formal a dining room feels. If it has a lot of trim work, high ceilings, pillars, or a larger crystal chandelier, it might be a challenge for those who love easy, casual style. On the flip side, if a room is just a plain box, indistinguishable from any other room in the house, it could be a head-scratcher for someone who wants a room that works with their dark-wood, Chippendale matching dining set.

SEVEN WAYS TO MAKE A FORMAL DINING ROOM FEEL MORE RELAXED

1. Paint it all white (trim and everything) to minimize the visual impact of formal millwork.
2. Paint it a playful, cheery color that doesn't allow the room to take itself too seriously.
3. Use an eclectic mix of furniture and avoid matching sets.
4. Replace a formal chandelier with something more casual or quirky, but make sure it still works with the scale of the room.
5. Don't use formal window treatments, but leave windows untreated (if privacy allows) or use informal alternatives like shutters or simple panels.
6. Use a casual rug like woven jute or cotton.

7. Use furniture pieces that are not traditionally seen in dining rooms, like a large bookcase filled with books and fun accessories or a wardrobe filled with folded quilts or favorite linens.

SEVEN WAYS TO MAKE A CASUAL DINING ROOM FEEL MORE FORMAL

1. Add picture frame molding, beams, or both (see pages 71 and 74).
2. Install hardwood floors. (They are easier to keep clean, anyway!)
3. Add a chandelier with lots of sparkle.
4. Use symmetry and visual repetition when arranging the furniture, art, and accessories.
5. Cover the walls in wallpaper or a mural
6. Use fabrics that feel luxurious, like velvet and linen, and patterns that are traditional, like chintz, damask, paisley, and toile.
7. Dress the windows in full-length drapes or curtains with swags.

OPPOSITE: This open-concept dining room in the Dietzmans' home was dressed up with the addition of a vintage crystal chandelier.

Curating *Tableware*

As I shared early in this chapter, I have a love for dishes, flatware, table linens, and serving pieces. I'm not sure where that came from. Maybe it was from admiring my Oma's dining room cabinets, filled with wedding silver and china. But I think it was probably more from my early days of going to yard sales and thrift stores. It was during an age of practicality when people didn't want to polish silver or iron linen. I could find beautiful pieces of silver and like-new sets of vintage napkins for practically nothing. A few cents, literally.

So the collection began. The advantage of buying tableware this way is that I ended up with an eclectic mix of pieces, creating my own custom set of dishes, my own mismatched flatware and glasses that were far more interesting (and less expensive) than a set purchased at the store. There were some common elements in the pieces I collected. Most were white, blue, or green, most were traditional patterns, but the thread that tied them all together was the fact that I selected them.

Selecting plates and glasses might feel like you're just buying something to meet a basic need (and you are), but it can be more than that. Each choice is a part of the curation and creation process of making your home uniquely yours. The aesthetic of a home doesn't consist of one larger decision, but of a thousand smaller decisions, and even the things you eat off and drink from add to that overall style.

MIX AND MATCH DISHES AND FLATWARE

One of the easiest ways to use formal pieces, like china and silver, in an informal way is to mix and match. Using matching sets is predictable and sets a more serious tone. Mixing patterns and colors, finishes and scale makes a table interesting, playful, and more expressive of your personality. Here are a few ways to break up those matching sets:

- Buy a few inexpensive solid-colored plates to pair with patterned dishes.
- Look for quirky bowls to layer over everyday plates.
- Use traditional dishes in unexpected ways, like serving ice cream or fruit salad out of a teacup.
- Mix in one utensil, like a spoon, from a pattern that differs from the other flatware. It can even be in a different material, like wood or metal.

† Give every person at the table a different china pattern. This can be an inexpensive way to buy fine china, one plate at a time, just purchasing the patterns you like. Orphaned pieces are often cheaper than individual pieces in a complete or larger set. I took this approach in collaboration with the mother of the bride for a wedding I designed, and I loved watching the guests admire and compare their plates. Each one was a little surprise to the person at that place.

TABLE LINENS

I am a textile junkie and love using napkins, tablecloths, runners, and even scraps of fabric, quilts, and blankets when adding softness to a table. Linens are another opportunity to further customize your table or buffet and invite your guests into something special.

I remember the first time I pulled out real plates and linen napkins to serve a group of teenagers who came over to eat at our house: they almost looked confused. One of the girls held up a folded and pressed linen napkin and asked, "Do we actually use these?" Yes! I had stacks and stacks of vintage linen napkins, so why not use them? I think most of the napkins went unused that night in favor of sleeves, but I think it made the kids feel special that they were cloth-napkin worthy!

I love classic white linen monogrammed napkins (I was fortunate to inherit some from my mother-in-law), but there are so many creative ways to customize cloth napkins to fit your personality:

† Collect napkins in different patterns and colors to make the experience more personal and playful.

† Have each member of the family stitch something on "their" napkin. I guarantee that kids will proudly want to use their creations. The design can be an initial, a memorable date, or a simple motif.

† Dye napkins in a color that coordinates with your decor. I dyed some stained antique napkins a beautiful indigo, and they were immediately transformed into something I would use more often.

† Cut up pretty cotton or linen fabric into large squares (an average dinner napkin is 22"–24" square) to make your own napkins out of a fabric you love. Use pinking shears to create a pretty edge that resists fraying, or create a double hem on each side to finish them off.

Project: HEIRLOOM HAND-STITCHED LINEN NAPKINS

WHAT YOU'LL NEED

- Linen cloth napkins (A typical set has six to twelve.)
- Embroidery floss in desired color
- Embroidery needle
- Embroidery hoop
- Scissors

A FEW HELPFUL TIPS

- As with most projects in this book, just relax! These do not have to be perfect. It's the personal touch and work done by hand that make them special. Human work is always imperfect work. I made six of these napkins and each one is a little different.
- You know the little strawberry that comes attached to the tomato pincushion? I always thought that was an adornment but recently learned it's filled with crushed walnut shells (or another similar material) to sharpen your needles! If your needle isn't moving through the fabric easily, insert it into the strawberry to make it sharp.
- A lovely alternate take on this idea is to have friends and family sign their names or initials in pencil and then embroider over their signature to make it permanent and washable. This idea can also be used on a tablecloth and can be added to by each guest who graces that table.

- This is a wonderful project to do as a family or with friends. Sewing circles were popular for a reason—they are a great opportunity for fellowship and conversation (without a screen as the mediator) while making something beautiful.

STEPS

1. Wash and iron the napkins.

2. Plan out your design. I selected a simple letter from a cross-stitch book that could be completed in an hour or less.

3. Cut a piece of embroidery floss 8"–12" long. Pull two threads from it, reserving the other four threads to use later. Thread the needle and double knot the end to prevent it from pulling through.

4. If needed, you can transfer your design onto the napkin with a pencil or transfer paper, but otherwise, simply follow the pattern and count the stitches. Using a nubby linen with a larger weave will make counting much easier.

5. If desired, put the work area into an embroidery hoop. This creates a tension in the fabric, making it easier to embroider. Use the embroidery needle and floss (two threads at a time) to stitch the design, following the pattern. Be mindful of the backs of the napkins, since they might be visible when the napkin is used. Try to keep the back as neat as possible.

6. Wash and iron again prior to use, if necessary.

1.

2.

5.

5.

Each hand-stitched napkin is slightly different, adding to the charm and homespun look.

bedrooms

---

bed·room

/'bed,rōōm, 'bed,rŏŏm/

noun

a room for sleeping in

YOU ARE EITHER IN YOUR BED OR IN YOUR SHOES, SO IT PAYS TO INVEST IN BOTH.
—JOHN WILDSMITH

The *Room* That No One Sees

"No one is going to see it but us." Jeff reminds me of that almost anytime I work on a project in our bedroom or bathroom. My response is always just as predictable. "Well, *I'll* see it." While I have regularly shared my home online since 2009, I've been decorating my personal spaces for my own enjoyment since I was a child, and it never occurred to me that it wasn't worth it because most people never saw it. My guess is that Jeff's sentiment is a common one, though.

In our current Minnesota home, all of the bedrooms were boxes with the required window, closet, and closing door. In our 1940s Pennsylvania house, the bedrooms were floored in pine, a more casual and less expensive material than the oak used in the downstairs common spaces, and the windows were small, the ceilings low. The rooms were just tucked under the sharply pitched roof of the one-and-a-half-story Cape Cod, unnoticed from the exterior of the home. What these cues tell me is bedrooms aren't very important. They are strictly a place to sleep and get dressed, and they often get the architectural and decorating leftovers, especially in a typical suburban house.

The trend in recent years is to make the master (or primary) bedroom bigger. It's still a box, but the room is massive, with big closets and a big bathroom. Bigger makes it better, right? The challenge when it comes to decorating and personalizing the average suburban bedroom is combating the box and making the rooms feel important and less like a default. The greater challenge may be giving ourselves permission to spend time and money on a space that is typically seen only by family members. It can feel frivolous for a room that "no one sees."

Bedrooms used to be some of the most important rooms in the house, with beds being a symbol of wealth and luxury. In medieval times, beds were so expensive and valuable, they would be recorded in a person's last will and testament to be passed down generation after generation. I'm sure there were many family fights over who got the bed! In this day and age, when cheap metal bed frames are common and used mattresses can't even be donated to a thrift store, it's hard to imagine such value being placed on a bed or the nondescript room it's inhabiting.

In this high-speed, technology-filled world, the personal, restful space of a bedroom is more important than ever. It's become so much more than just a place to sleep and to store your clothes. It's a sanctuary, and it's worth making it feel like a cocoon, comfortable and rejuvenating, tailored and fitted, even if it's just for you.

The Good News of the *Blank Box*

I am being a little hard on the boxy suburban bedroom. While rooms with lots of character and charm built into their bones are my preference, "the box" has one major benefit—it's a blank canvas. It is just waiting for creativity and ingenuity to bring those walls to life. It's deliciously brimming with potential.

While the style of the house might be boldly represented in the common rooms, bedrooms tend to be pretty neutral. This means the style of the room's occupant can be the top consideration. Bedrooms can be a departure from the rest of the house since they are private spaces and generally more isolated. They are a great opportunity to try out new ideas and feel the freedom to make a departure from the primary style of the house. If you sense that you're fighting the style of your home, the bedrooms might be the easiest place to start injecting your personality!

FIVE WAYS TO TAKE A BEDROOM BEYOND THE BLANK BOX

ONE: GET A BED

And I don't mean a metal frame to hold up a box spring and mattress! There are only a few valid excuses for having a metal bed frame as an adult: (1) You want one. *Okay, I'll allow it.* (2) You move a lot. *Understandable.* (3) You still live in a college dorm. *Naturally.* (4) You're saving up for a bed frame that's an actual piece of furniture. *Smart.* I am being a bit facetious here and I'm sure there are more valid reasons, but I want to encourage you to get a bed frame that is a real piece of furniture. In most bedrooms, the bed is the focal point, and a bed frame can add structure and interest and define the style better than almost anything else. If you don't take another thing I say away from this chapter, I hope you'll decide to treat yourself to a real bed frame that you love.

TWO: BE THOUGHTFUL ABOUT STORAGE PIECES

Dressers are another default when it comes to bedrooms. *Well, I need a place to put my clothes, so I'll buy a dresser.* I thought that way for years until I swapped out my dresser for a wardrobe with shelves installed, and I will never go back. I can see all of my folded clothes, and my T-shirts aren't stuffed into a drawer! Be thoughtful about the storage pieces you use, and question every choice. *Is this what really works for me? Is this what I need to store my stuff, or is this a default choice? Would something else be better?* In fact, you might not need clothes storage outside of your closet, and the space can be used as a sitting area, a place to stretch out on the floor in the morning, or a quiet corner for a writing desk.

THREE: USE BEAUTIFUL TEXTILES

A bedroom provides a fantastic opportunity to use a lot of fabrics, blankets, pillows, and textiles. Bedrooms by nature and function should be soft and inviting. This is a prime room in which to use layers of fabric patterns and textures along with comfortable bedding and an overstuffed chair with a place to put up your feet. If you're going to put your decorating dollars in one place in the bedroom, put it in the bed, mattress, quality sheets, and bedding. You'll sleep better and your room will look polished.

OPPOSITE: The feature wall behind the bed may look like wallpaper, but it's actually starched fabric! A tutorial for this technique starts on page 144.

An antique French wardrobe, purchased off of an online marketplace for $400, provides more efficient storage than a dresser and better fits the scale of the large room.

FOUR: DESIGN YOUR LIGHTING

I think it's fair to say that most suburban bedrooms will have one overhead light and it's typically a flush-mount, builder-grade fixture (or a ceiling fan if you live in a warmer climate). This is a perfect place to add a custom fixture not only for its design, but also for the kind of light it casts. Installing a dimmer switch is also an easy and inexpensive upgrade that allows low, ambient light when needed. Supplement the ceiling fixture with task lighting for reading as well as ambient lighting and night-lights where they are needed for safety.

FIVE: SPRUCE UP THE WALLS

I'm going to beat the drum about customizing your walls all through this book! The big box can be put into submission by adding depth, texture, structure, and detail with wood, fabric, paint, and more. The walls truly are a blank canvas on which your style can be displayed.

Project: STARCHED FABRIC WALL

As a military brat, I watched my mom get very creative with decorating a nine-hundred-square-foot apartment that was basically a rental. It was maybe even a step down from a rental in that my parents didn't choose it. They were assigned to it and had to do their best to make it feel like home.

We couldn't paint the walls or make any permanent changes, so my mom used faux butcher-block contact paper to cover Army-issue-green counters and starched a cherry-brown-and-white German folk art fabric to an ugly metal partition in the bathroom. I didn't think anything of it as a kid, because it was just where we lived, but I look back at it as an adult and am impressed with her ingenuity.

Starching fabric to the walls was apparently a well-known trick often used by military wives. Some used that treatment on entire rooms! The reason it was so popular was that it was a relatively easy and inexpensive way to transform a room, but it was also entirely removable. It just peels right off without damaging the walls. And, as a bonus, the fabric can be washed and repurposed!

As an adult, I've used this trick several times, and it's always been successful and stunning. I'm surprised more people don't know about it, but I'm always flooded with questions and surprised comments when I share that the "wallpaper" on my walls isn't paper at all, but fabric stuck in place with a common household product—liquid starch.

WHAT YOU'LL NEED

- Enough fabric to cover the desired area (plus extra to allow for lining up the pattern)
- Quart bottles of liquid starch (Plan on using one bottle for every three to four panels.)
- Tape measure
- Pencil
- Level
- Paint tray and plastic tray liner
- Paint roller
- ⅜"-nap roller cover
- 2½" angled sash brush
- Sharp sewing scissors or rotary cutter
- Cutting mat
- Yardstick
- Thumbtacks
- Utility knife with extra blades
- Metal putty knife
- Stepladder

2.

A FEW HELPFUL TIPS

- You can use any kind of fabric for this technique, from lightweight cotton and linen to a heavier woven fabric.
- If this is your first time hanging fabric or wallpaper, I would suggest selecting a busy, allover pattern and staying away from stripes, checks, or plaids. The former option is much more forgiving. The latter can clearly show if your measurements are off or your pattern isn't straight.
- Thumbtacks are your friend! Use them to hold the fabric in place while you're lining up the pattern and cutting around windows and doors. This simple trick will save a lot of frustration!
- This project can be done solo, but it's easier if you have an extra set of hands to pass the roller when you're up on the ladder, etc.
- The more starch, the better! It will be drippy and a little messy, but it washes up easily with water. The fabric won't adhere to the wall well if it's not soaked with starch. I use a roller to control the mess, but my mom completely submerged each panel in a bucket of starch!
- Work on the project in sections. You're likely to do quality work if you're not rushing through the project or working when you're fatigued and sick of hanging fabric! This also means you can move furniture away from one wall at a time and move it right back when you're done, causing less upheaval. Wash the brush and roller with water between uses.
- The fabric will look darker when wet, but it will lighten again as it dries.

STEPS

1. PREP THE WALL. Make sure the wall is clean and free from any nails or screws and patch any holes. Remove outlet and light-switch plates. Proceed to either step 2 or 3 depending on the area you're covering. (Safety note: If you're using this treatment on a wall with electrical outlets or switches, turn off the power to that room at the breaker when applying starch and fabric around the outlets. This will ensure safety and prevent the possibility of being shocked when working with wet hands around an electrical source.)

2. IF HANGING THE FABRIC ON A FEATURE WALL, like behind a bed, use a tape measure to determine the wall width and find the center point. Mark the center with a pencil. Measure and mark a distance that is half of the fabric's width to the left of the wall's center point. (For example, if the fabric is 52" wide once the raw edges are trimmed, make a mark 26" to the left of the center point. Place the level vertically on this mark and make a plumb line [vertical line] from floor to ceiling.) This line will be used as a guide when hanging the first fabric panel, which will be centered on your wall.

3. IF HANGING THE FABRIC IN THE ENTIRE ROOM, START IN A CORNER THAT IS LESS VISIBLE. This is typically behind the entrance to the room. Mark a plumb line with a level where you want the fabric panel to start. It's important that this line is plumb, since all of the other panels will be lined up from this first panel Tip: Don't start in the corner of a wall, but 1"–2" inside or outside of the corner. This will make for a neater seam if the cut isn't directly in the corner.

6.

6.

6.

6.

4. CUT YOUR FIRST FABRIC PANEL AND TRIM THE RAW EDGES. Since you don't have a pattern to match yet, cut your piece of fabric to the proper length. Remove the fabric's raw edges using scissors or a rotary cutter, cutting mat, and a yardstick or straight edge. All cuts need to be as straight as possible. Don't worry about fraying, which will happen. Any stray threads can be tamed with the starch. Measure the wall's height (minus any trim, like baseboards or crown molding) and add a few inches to this measurement to allow a little wiggle room.

5. APPLY THE STARCH TO THE WALL. Pour liquid starch into a lined paint tray, then roll the starch onto the section of wall that will be covered with the first fabric panel. This entire section should be liberally covered with starch. Wipe up any drips with a damp paper towel or rag.

6. INSTALL THE FIRST FABRIC PANEL. Using a stool or stepladder to stand on, line up the precut panel's top corner with the plumb line. Tack the fabric in place to prevent it from falling off while you're working. Smooth out the fabric, working in a downward motion to adhere it to the wall. Smooth any wrinkles or folds by hand. Slide the fabric, if necessary, to make sure it's square to the ceiling or crown molding and straight along the plumb line. Once the panel is properly placed, roll over the entire panel liberally with starch.

7. TRIM EXCESS FABRIC AND SMOOTH THE EDGES. Use a sharp utility knife with a fresh blade and a straight edge to trim excess fabric from the ceiling, along molding, and carefully around outlets, switches, and vents. Use a putty knife behind the blade to hold the edge in place and protect the walls and trim. If the fabric is snagging or pulling, it's time to change the blade. Apply starch over the edges with a 2½" angled sash brush and smooth any frayed threads with your fingers.

8. APPLY SUBSEQUENT PANELS. Make a note of the pattern and where you need to cut the next panel to allow it to line up. Repeat steps 4–7 with the second panel, matching the pattern with the first. Repeat this process with the remaining panels. If the room you're working in isn't plumb or level (which most aren't), you may notice the pattern shifting along the ceiling. Just account for those changes when you're cutting the panels so you don't come up short! You should always have at least a little fabric to trim along the ceiling to create a nice, straight line. The panels will dry in a few hours.

6.

7.

7.

7.

STARCHED FABRIC

- ⊰ Home decor fabric comes in 54″ widths, which can be difficult to maneuver when hanging on your own, but the extra width means you cover more ground with each panel.
- ⊰ The stretch in the fabric makes lining up the pattern a more forgiving process.
- ⊰ Some fabrics will fray when cut with a utility knife.
- ⊰ It's easy to clean with a vacuum.
- ⊰ It can be peeled off the wall in minutes, without any damage to the drywall.

Our *Bespoke* Bedroom

Our bedroom was one of those "bigger is better" suburban master suites, but I am not complaining about that. After arguing with my older brother in every move about who got the bigger bedroom, I finally have the biggest bedroom ever! Well, not ever, but it's the biggest bedroom I've ever had by a mile. It's so big that our queen-sized bed looked dinky. Almost all of the furniture we brought from our last bedroom looked out of scale in this one. The challenge with our last master bedroom was that it was long and skinny with one small, awkwardly placed window. The challenge with this bedroom is how big it is.

Big means more space to fill physically and visually. It was a challenge for me, because I honed my decorating skills in relatively small spaces. I can do cozy, quaint, comfy, and snug. Big was new.

Wallpaper *versus* Starched Fabric

WALLPAPER

- ⊰ It is relatively rigid and comes in smaller widths (typically 20″–24″), so it's easier to manage when hanging.
- ⊰ When it is wet, wallpaper paste adheres to the wall but still allows you to shift the piece you're hanging to line up the pattern.
- ⊰ It's easy to cut with a utility knife.
- ⊰ It's easy to clean with a damp cloth.
- ⊰ Even modern papers with primer underneath can be a pain to remove (unless it's peel and stick).

But I do love a good challenge! It took me about three years to get this room figured out and to find the right pieces to fill the space. It started by upsizing to a king bed, which clearly this room was designed to accommodate. Immediately, the bed was the star of the show, balanced out by the French wardrobe purchased on Craigslist a few years before we moved.

I sold the smaller washstands I was using for bedside tables and replaced them with antique dressers. One I already had, and one I purchased at a local secondhand shop. The scale of the dressers worked much better with the bed and the room.

A chaise slipcovered in inexpensive linen fills the corner by the wardrobe and creates a little reading nook. The rest of the pieces were patient finds. An 1800s melodeon case (it's a type of organ) was the perfect fit for the wall between the closet and bathroom. It's beefed up visually by some antique shutters flanked by ironstone platters. A rocking horse that I hand painted to look old sits on top. The antique Jenny Lind daybed under the window was a lucky find on a local marketplace. I had been looking for something exactly like that for months and finally found it for one hundred dollars. I hopped in the car as soon as I could to pay for it and take it home!

To customize the bones of the room, I painted it in Stonington Gray by Benjamin Moore (this room started the love of that particular color for me), installed a chair rail and picture frame molding (see tutorial for that on page 71), and replaced the old ceiling fan in favor of an antique chandelier. And to make the bed even more of a feature, I made a bed crown (also called a tester or half canopy). It might be a little flouncy or over-the-top for some, but I love how it frames out the bed and ties in with the toile curtain fabric. And I am not afraid to go unabashedly pretty in certain rooms.

A big part of customizing our bedroom involved sewing, and I believe this is one of the tricks to breaking out of the store-bought look. I sewed the curtains, all of the pillows, the bed crown, and all of the slipcovers. Being able to sew makes my fabric options almost limitless, and I can make those fabrics work well together by combining them on key pieces, like the center pillow on the bed. I don't love sewing. It's probably my least favorite DIY activity, but I do it because it gives me the flexibility to create what I envision in my head.

Assignment:
CUSTOMIZE WITHOUT SEWING

If you don't sew (and don't want to give it a try), create a custom look by mixing and matching pillows, curtains, and other textiles instead of using a matching set. This mix-and-match look will create a room that is more personal and unique. You can always start with one or two patterns and allow the look to evolve from there. You can even change it out with the seasons!

TIPS FOR DECORATING A BIG BEDROOM

- Pay attention to scale! As was true with the queen-sized bed in our huge bedroom, pieces will shrink and look dinky when they aren't large enough for the space they are trying to fill. This is true of furniture and accessories.
- Use trim work, like a chair rail, chunky crown molding, or an interesting ceiling treatment to make the room feel cozier.
- Maximize the space by using it for different functions. You can set up an entire seating area, a place to exercise, a reading nook, or a writing desk. (I would suggest keeping desks for work out of the bedroom, since that can be stressful. This desk is just for journaling, sketching, and writing letters.)
- Get creative with art! Use large-scale pieces that cover a lot of wall space, or group small items together to make them visually larger collectively than they would be individually.
- Be patient. It can be easy to feel pressured by a large, half-empty room. Just because the space is big doesn't mean you need to fill it all at once. Take your time and find the right pieces for the room.
- Watch the clutter. I know this is important in a small space and we'll get to that in a minute, but it's so easy to let stuff get out of hand when you have tons of space. A big room, big closet, or ample cabinet space doesn't have to be filled just because it's there.

TIPS FOR DECORATING A SMALL BEDROOM

- Again, pay attention to scale. Massive pieces are going to crowd a small room, making it feel even smaller. It's like wearing pants that are too tight!
- Look for pieces that have maximum storage and a small footprint. Every piece matters, so be very picky about the size and function.
- There is a myth that you can't paint small rooms in dark colors or use busy patterns. You can do both. Some of my favorite rooms featured in magazines are small bedrooms wrapped wall-to-wall in toile. There is something about the busyness of the fabric that adds depth, and the same is true with dark colors. It turns a small space into a little jewel box.
- Use mirrors to reflect light and add visual depth.
- Eliminate pieces that take up floor space, and opt for pieces that can be hung on the wall. For example, swap a freestanding full-length mirror with one that hangs on the wall or the back of a door, and trade a floor lamp for a wall sconce.
- Keep the clutter under control. I think it's easier to be mindful of clutter when you're in a small house, so every piece that comes into that small room should be intentional...down to your socks.

Guest Rooms

If bedrooms in general get the leftovers of the house, then the guest room gets the leftovers of the leftovers! I'm not going to knock that, because it makes sense. It's a room that's not used as often as bedrooms occupied by the family, so it gets the hand-me-down dresser with the wonky drawers and the bed with the old mattress. Your in-laws can endure that for a couple of nights, right? If your decorating budget is limited, I would suggest putting your money toward the rooms you use most. But just because a room is made with leftovers doesn't mean it has to look like it!

Believe it or not, our guest room is outfitted with mostly leftovers as well. The bed is our old queen bed that was displaced when we upsized to a king. The bedside dressers were both purchased secondhand for about $150, and the wing chair was a free yard sale leftover that I slipcovered. The wardrobe was the only piece of furniture I purchased deliberately for that room, and the room's yellow-and-beige color scheme was designed around that piece and the gold bedding I had in our last guest room. The wardrobe was my statement piece!

Guest rooms can be a delightful place to explore color palettes and design styles that are a departure from the norm. I stepped away from my beloved blue and white to create a room that is neutral and warm. Neutral, but not boring! A guest room is also the perfect place to step out on a limb with something like wallpaper or an allover wall treatment like beadboard, paneling, or decorative painting. Since it's not a frequently used room, you're not likely to get tired of it.

Decorating aside, I think great guest rooms are

comfortable and welcoming. This means that the room is outfitted with basic necessities and a few extras to make your guests feel pampered.

CREATING AN INVITING GUEST ROOM

⚭ **A comfortable bed and bedding.** Try sleeping on your guest bed for a few nights and see how it feels. If it's hard as a rock or lumpy or sagging, it's time to save up for a replacement. At the very least, add a mattress topper for some cushion or support. Also, use sheets that feel nice, and offer pillows with a couple of different shape and thickness options. On our guest

which is much cooler than the rest of the house, so we even have an electric blanket as an option. On the flip side, keeping a fan in the closet is also a thoughtful touch if the room is too warm or your guest sleeps best with ambient white noise.

⧓ Leave a few empty drawers, if possible, so guests have an option to unpack.

Kids' Rooms

Kids' bedrooms really could be an entire chapter or an entire book! The needs and decor tastes of kids evolve almost yearly, especially when they are young. Because it's such a big topic, I almost didn't include it at all, but I know many people who read this book will have kids or grandkids who live with them or visit frequently and might want some tips geared specifically to those rooms. When decorating a kid's room, the most important thing to remember is that it belongs to him or her. Yes, it's in your house, and yes, some boundaries are needed, but ultimately, it is their space and it needs to reflect their personality. As someone who loves to decorate and has two boys who do not like antiques and really do not want me to decorate their rooms, I find that's a tough thing for me! But I am embracing it and, as they've gotten older, I'm treating them like design clients.

bed, I have a couple of pillows that are thicker and firmer and a couple that are feather-filled, soft, and flat. (Be mindful of the laundry detergent you use, too, since some people are sensitive or even allergic to strong-smelling soaps and fabric softeners.)

⧓ Keep at least one outlet free for guests to use for charging their electronic devices. Having extra chargers or extension cords in the drawers of the nightstand is a nice bonus.

⧓ Have reading lamps on both sides of the bed. Since the lamps in our guest room aren't within reach, we have them plugged into a switch that works on a remote.

⧓ Keep plenty of extra blankets and towels on hand. Our guest room is in the basement,

HOW TO BE THE DESIGNER
FOR YOUR KIDS

- Ask them what they want. If your kids are anything like mine, they will be all over the place and their answers might change each time you talk to them about it! Your job as the designer is to be a filter, to take those ideas and do a little bit of problem-solving to see what will work and what won't. During the idea stage, it helps to look at photos. Just like adults, sometimes kids don't really know what they want, but they know what they like when they see it.

- Play the hot-cold game with decor. Is this room, accessory, or bedding set getting warmer or cooler? Turning what they are drawn to and what they dislike into a game might make the process more fun and engaging, especially for younger kids.

- Have some defined boundaries. With my boys, I told them we weren't going to do over-the-top themed rooms, simply because what they are into changes too frequently. The foundations of the room won't be designed around characters. Those can show up in art and accessories. Figure out what your boundaries are. It's their room, but it's your house.

- Allow them to participate in all of the choices from the wall color to the furniture. For my boys, I didn't give them the entire paint deck and tell them to pick a color. We talked about colors first, and then I showed them a few paint chips that worked with what they described and I also knew would look nice. A good designer will do that for their client—allow limited choices in order to make sure the choices aren't going to end up looking garish or crazy. My sons like

midcentury modern (go figure), so I would find secondhand furniture pieces online (that I vetted first for price, size, and quality) and then allowed them to have a final say. We ended up with a really cool midcentury-modern dresser for Calvin for fifty dollars using this method.

- When the bones of the room are in place, let your kids decorate. I love watching my boys, who don't care very much about decorating and design, arrange stuff on dressers and shelves. It's a way to see what's important to them and what looks aesthetically pleasing in their eyes. Don't worry if it's "right" or how you would do it. They're kids for only a few precious years, and soon you can turn their rooms into offices and hobby rooms!

Assignment:
RELIVE YOUR
CHILDHOOD

Talk to your kids about your childhood bedroom. What did you enjoy the most? What would you have done differently? What did you wish your parents allowed? A swing? A fort? Red walls? Thinking about your own experience through the lens of a kid or teenager will help you be open and understanding during the process. Your kids might get some great ideas for their own rooms based on your stories.

- Above all, have fun. Especially if you love decorating, which I'm going to assume you have some interest in if this book ended up in your hands. It's so important to share that love with your kids in a way that is fun. If you're frustrated and forcing your ideas on them, they aren't going to enjoy it. The relationship, the experience, is always, always more important than the stuff and the room.

The *Intentional* Bedroom

In his book *Essentialism*, Greg McKeown states, "If you don't prioritize your life, someone else will." I think the same idea is true of rooms. If you don't prioritize what is in them and, more importantly, what's not in them, then clutter seems to migrate in and multiply. You'll end up with hand-me-downs that no one wanted, including you. It's the last-minute dumping ground when company comes over. It's where the laundry piles up and the vacuum is parked. You eventually start to live at the mercy of your stuff.

That is what happens when we don't prioritize what comes into our homes and specific spaces. That is what happens when we're unintentional about what we buy, what we say yes to, and how we store and use those things. And that happens to even the tidiest people! We get busy, stuff piles up, we're occupied with other things, we rush into decisions, we don't think things through, we buy on impulse, and it ends up showing in a room that doesn't feel thoughtfully curated, cohesive, or customized.

I think this is particularly important to pay attention to in personal, restful spaces. Whatever restful looks like to you, that's what your room should be.

Assignment:
CREATE YOUR SANCTUARY

Write a list of things and places that evoke calm and peace to you. Maybe it's water, the color blue, a white space, no visible clutter, pan flute, cozy and dark, flannel...The list can be as random, purposeful, general, or specific as you want. The point is to not overthink it but to write down the things you associate with comfort and rest. This list should be your guide when creating your sanctuary. Fill the room with the textures, colors, smells, and sounds that tell all of your senses it's time to rest. And, perhaps more importantly, remove things that are not restful to you.

When creating your sanctuary, take some time to reflect on what feels restful to you. Whatever your idea of a restful space is, pursue that. Be intentional about that. And be a ruthless gatekeeper.

CREATIVE & WORK

spaces

The statistics I found in my research varied, but all of the articles I read about working from home confirmed that more people are working from home now than ever before. In addition, more kids are doing their schoolwork at home through either homeschooling or remote learning. And more people are starting their own businesses out of their homes, too! All of this means that we need space in our homes to accommodate these task-oriented activities. We need offices, studios, workshops, and rooms for studying, learning, creating, and making. This means we also need the space and storage capacity to house all of the gear we need to accomplish those tasks. Sometimes it's as simple as a flat work surface and a comfortable chair, but other times it requires dedicating an entire room to a specific function or multiple functions.

When my family moved to our home in Minnesota, we knew it would need to accommodate my business in addition to housing our family. In Pennsylvania I'd been working out of a 2,500-square-foot studio that was separate from my house, and now I needed to fit all of the functions performed there into a typical suburban home. Working on the dining room table just wasn't going to be practical. Photo shoots, video production, furniture makeovers, upholstery, styling and staging, and design work all had to find a place in our new home. That was going to be a tall order.

When I picked out our current home as a strong contender during internet searches, I initially thought the walk-out basement would become my work space. I could use the downstairs family room as my main work area and the smaller room for storage. (Photography and upholstery specifically can come with a lot of supplies and bulky gear.) Once our offer was extended and accepted and we started to make more specific plans, we recognized that the family room would be an important living space. It would be

a hangout for the boys when friends came over and a place for us to pile on a generously sized sectional for our pizza and movie night each Friday. If possible, we needed to find other spaces for my business.

The smallest of the upstairs bedrooms could be my sewing room, which would house my upholstery supplies, sewing machines, and fabric stash. The home office off the foyer could obviously be my office. But I also needed a space for photoshoots and creative work that was separate from my office. Fortunately, our house had a three-season porch (really, it's a one-, maybe two-season porch since it's located in Minnesota) that was brimming with possibility.

A small upstairs bedroom is used as a sewing room with the addition of a wardrobe to hold fabric and a pine desk to act as a sewing table. An antique French daybed makes the room functional as a guest room as well.

My *Bespoke* Studio

"You're going to hate it." Those were the words Jeff said to me about the mystery room located off the kitchen of our potential new house in Rochester. We could initially see only a sliver of it through a glass door off the kitchen in the real estate listing, but our realtor took a few pictures of it for us and sent them along to Jeff. We could now see it was an unfinished "three-season" sunporch clad in dark cedar paneling, topped off with a sagging, dusty ceiling fan.

Jeff was wrong. My heart leaped when I envisioned every surface painted in a shade of white to reflect the light from the south-facing windows. "It's a perfect studio!" He wasn't convinced, but he's learned to trust my eye when it comes to seeing potential in things that other people overlook.

When the house became ours, the studio was the first room we started working on since I needed a studio for my work. We primed and painted every single surface and removed the bent and dusty blinds. We also had it insulated and climate-controlled so I would be able to use it year-round. (I really appreciated that during the polar vortex of 2019, when the thermometer bottomed out at around minus thirty degrees!)

The studio is a sanctuary and, even though it's not large or grand, it's been everything I've needed it to be. It's a hardworking space that shifts from acting as a backdrop for videos and photos to an art and design studio and a place to record podcasts. It's accommodating as I follow my curiosity and continue to evolve as a creative and entrepreneur.

The focal point of the studio is most certainly the large antique cabinet. I purchased the hardware counter from a Craigslist ad in Maryland and a bookcase that was removed from a schoolhouse in Minnesota and paired them to make one large storage unit that houses my resource books and art supplies. It was a risk that paid off by providing a strong focal point for the room and loads of practicality.

We also built a closet to house bulky equipment that was scattered in storage spaces all over the house. It was important to me that my business didn't take over the house and I could keep professional and private spaces as separate as possible. Building a large closet gave me the space to house all of my gear in a room allocated for work.

A sunporch off the kitchen was finished and insulated to be used as an art studio. Gallons of paint transformed the dark-wood walls, ceiling, and floor into a light and airy space.

The remaining pieces of furniture are on casters and sliders so they can be rearranged or moved as need or whim dictates. The goal, though, is to make every piece count. Each stick of furniture has to provide much-needed storage and contribute to the overall creative ambience. To me, that is at the heart of customizing a work space. Every piece matters. Every detail *matters*. All of the pieces work together to create a space that is conducive to production. That's been my goal, anyway, as I've created functional and inspiring work spaces in my own home.

Creating Work Zones

Most home offices are approached with some sort of assumption about the basic needs. A desk, a chair, a credenza or bookcase, etc. I want to challenge you, though, to really think through the work you do and break it down into individual tasks that make up a typical day. This is important so your work space can be designed around those tasks. This might mean arranging the room in a specific way or just arranging your desk so the things you use most are readily accessible.

Organize the list of your individual tasks into groups of like tasks. For example, divide the work into things done on the computer, things done on the phone, work that involves writing, creative work, reading, etc. In my case, I was able to divide most of my tasks into four buckets:

1. **COMPUTER/BUSINESS**
2. **CREATIVE**
3. **DIY PROJECTS/FURNITURE REFINISHING**
4. **SEWING/UPHOLSTERY**

I then designed my work spaces to create a zone for each of these tasks. The home office is my "computer/business" zone. This is where I pay bills, respond to e-mails, write, edit photos, work on planning and strategy, etc. When I go to that office, I know it's time to buckle down and get to work. I do have a few pleasant distractions for when I get stuck, like an inspiration board, a library of decorating, design, and business books, and my guitar.

My studio is my creative space, and everyone in the family knows that when Mom is in there creating, door closed and music playing, they need to leave me alone unless they are on fire. Well, or unless there is something very important. It's not a space for clutter unless it's my creative clutter and not a space for roughhousing unless it's my own creative play and I'm getting a little wild with the paint. It's a sacred, creative space. And I have to be disciplined about keeping it that way. I have all but banned my computer from the room unless I'm doing creative work on it. If I want to work on e-mail or planning, I need to physically pick up my laptop and walk across the house to my office.

This might sound silly and unnecessary. *Does it really matter which room you're sitting in?* Yes, it actually does. We take cues from our surroundings, and one of the secrets of being a prolific creative is ritual. The room we're in, the things that surround us, the sounds and smells are all cues. We really don't notice them unless we

pay attention. One of the best things I did for my creativity was to establish those zones and rituals within those zones to cue my brain: It's time to write. It's time to paint. It's time to plan. When I step into my studio, I immediately feel that creative vibe. It can suck me in for hours.

I take it even further than that and have a playlist for painting, a playlist for writing, and a couple of different playlists for home projects. The music motivates me or gets me in a right, focused frame of mind. I have a candle I burn when I'm writing as well—Charlotte Brontë by Oldfield Society. Even the subtle smell is a cue.

Sewing takes place in the sewing room, and my DIY projects mostly happen in the garage or outside. Those zones aren't as protected or important, because the work I'm doing doesn't require as much mental space, creativity, or concentration. I can do that sort of work when my kids are wrestling in the next room or asking for me to make them "second breakfast" during a break from school (when they seemingly eat all day and forget that the kitchen isn't a locked room that only Mom can open).

Work zones aren't only a cue to you, but a cue to your family, which can help with creating healthy boundaries between work and life. That is so important when you work from home.

If you don't have entirely separate rooms to create work zones, create them within one room. This technique is on display in classrooms across the US. The reading zone has a bookcase and beanbag chairs, the desks are personal space for lessons and independent work, etc. Divide one room into imaginary zones you can move between. A chair for reading, a smaller writing desk for non-computer work, a drafting table, etc.

Creating zones and rituals around your work has the potential to be the secret weapon to maximizing your available space and making you more effective at your job when working, learning, and creating from home. In addition, it can support your being more present during family time and intentional about rest.

Customizing *New Office Furniture*

I absolutely love antiques and will use them at every opportunity I get. But there are times when buying a new piece is better and more functional. After using several antique desks and desk chairs, I have learned this is the case with office furniture. Antique furniture was obviously not made to accommodate computers, and old desk chairs tend to be smaller in scale and are often tipping hazards. I fought with my office furniture for years until I finally relented and got a new desk and proper desk chair for my home office. It made such a difference having a file drawer that fits hanging file folders and an ample work surface.

I generally don't like an off-the-shelf look, though! I want to put my touch on just about everything that comes into my home, so I've customized the new pieces to make them uniquely mine.

I share more detail and some of these same ideas in the chapter on furniture (chapter XI), but here are some office-specific ideas for customizing new furniture:

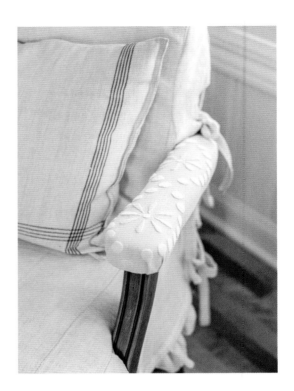

- SLIPCOVERS: I slipcovered both of the run-of-the-mill desk chairs I bought for my studio and home office in antique linens. This is a great way to make a desk chair fit a specific aesthetic or just look more appropriate in a home.
- REPLACING HARDWARE: I almost always replace hardware on new pieces! They often come with inexpensive, nondescript handles, so I'll select antique hardware or pulls and knobs that better fit my style. It's a job that usually takes ten to fifteen minutes and a screwdriver.
- PAINT: I usually don't paint brand-new pieces of furniture, but it is always an option! Sometimes you find just the right piece at an amazing price, but it's absolutely the wrong color or finish. Look for pieces that are solid wood so they can be sanded and painted or stripped and refinished. Solid wood pieces will also last much longer than their particleboard counterparts.
- UNCONVENTIONAL USES: Sometimes you don't have to alter the appearance of a piece to customize it, but just alter its intended function. A large dining table can become an

The Organized
Work Space

Organization is paramount when it comes to work spaces. Now, I want to insert that organization looks different for everyone. For some, it's about tidiness, order, labels, clean surfaces, and color-coding. For others, organization is piles and stacks, where everything is out in the open, on display, and readily at hand, which looks completely chaotic to someone who doesn't understand the system. Organization isn't about uniform neatness. It's about being able to work joyfully in your own space. It's about removing distractions and visual to-do lists that come with having things out of place. It's about making your work the priority of the work space over the stuff that's in it.

expansive work surface, a small dresser can be a printer stand, an artist's easel can hold an inspiration board or whiteboard, an entire desk can be built into a large wardrobe or armoire. There is so much potential when you push yourself to think outside the box.

If you're buying new office furniture on a budget, look for businesses that are closing and selling the contents of their office. Legal and accounting firms specifically tend to have beautiful solid wood furniture!

TIPS ON ORGANIZING A WORKSPACE

1. **IDENTIFY THE NEEDS.** Every type of work is going to have different storage requirements. Take a moment to really think through yours. Do you need a filing cabinet? A desk? Do you need small storage, like a piece with lots of tiny drawers for meticulously sorting small tools and materials? Or do you need a large closet for bulky gear? Identify your storage needs so they can be met.

2. **BE HONEST ABOUT HOW YOU ORGANIZE.** In order to create a space that really works for you, it's important to understand and acknowledge how you work. You're not doing

yourself any favors by spending a day putting things into bins and containers if you are not someone who is going to continue to put things in bins and containers. If you get overwhelmed by visual mess, open storage might be too much maintenance and distraction.

3. **MAKE IT EASY.** A system of organizing should serve you. You should not be a slave to the system. If it's not easy, it won't work long-term and will be more of a frustration than a help. It doesn't have to be easy for anyone else. It just has to work for you.

4. **TAKE NOTES.** Pay attention as you move through the space. Where are the bottlenecks? What slows you down? What pulls you out of a focused zone? Make notes of those bottlenecks and address them next time you're cleaning your work space.

5. **KEEP SHORT ACCOUNTS.** If you're not familiar with this saying, it's a financial slogan that means to reconcile your accounts and pay or collect your balances regularly. It's also a spiritual saying meaning "to confess regularly." It's about not letting things get out of hand. In a work space, it means making organizing a regular part of your job. It's an opportunity to tweak things that aren't working and address problem areas we all have. It can prevent you from becoming overwhelmed.

WORK SPACE REVIEW

Organization in a work space is a part of customization. If you've ever sat at someone else's desk to get some work done, you intuitively start to customize the space. You move the pen jar to the other side, you adjust the chair, scoot a stack of papers out of the way. You start to make mini-customizations so the work can begin. In our own spaces that we use daily, though, we can become oblivious to the things that don't work because we've simply learned how to adapt around them. Take time once a year to reassess your work spaces and question how they are working or even *if* they are working.

I've done this review regularly in my work spaces as my work has changed and evolved, and it's helped those spaces change and evolve with me. With each new creative endeavor, I can address the storage and space requirements for those tasks, making them feel like a more integrated part of my job. It also helps me to let go of things that worked well once but are no longer serving me.

ADDING PERSONALITY TO HARDWORKING SPACES

As we've established, function comes first in a home office. But that doesn't mean outfitting the room has to stop there. That really is just the beginning. To customize my own home office over the past three years, I've slowly worked on the large functional pieces—a work surface paired with the right chair, storage for my books and office supplies. Arranging and rearranging things until the needs were met efficiently. All

through this process, I kept aesthetics in mind like the lighting, the position of the furniture in relation to the window, and the flow of the traffic path.

After tweaking and adjusting, the bones of the room were right and it was time to inject some personality. We had already changed out the fourteen-year-old carpet for hardwood floors, and painted the trim a bright white and the walls a soft blue gray. I was ready to add more layers and personality. For a few months I marinated on what that would look like. Would it be a painted wall treatment? Picture frame molding, as we've done in other rooms in the house? Tone-on-tone stripes? I didn't find my answer until I was at a local hardware store purchasing wood for another project.

I spotted inexpensive faux wood paneling with a random vertical beaded detail. The color and finish were all wrong, a dated beige wood grain that looked like it belonged in a 1970s ranch, but I knew it would look fantastic painted. It reminded me of traditional office paneling, which would suit my house, the room, and my style. As it was only $20 per panel, I would also be able to clad the room for $160, which was a lot of bang for the decorating buck.

I made an on-the-spot decision to go for it, went home and measured, and picked up the panels later that day. I painted the newly installed paneling in a crisp, bright white to keep the room fresh and visually quiet. It looked great, but I wanted just a little more. After much internal debate (it's funny how some choices are easy and others cause so much angst), I opted to install a blue-and-white wallpaper with a Swedish vibe above the paneling. It provided a backdrop that

The Dietzmans gave their porch a makeover so it could be used as a creative work space for Cheri.

added personality and character to the room without being busy or distracting. The room feels like the perfect combination of stimulating and inspiring and a calming breath of fresh air. I finished the room off with some of my own artwork, a gilded inspiration board, and a few accessories that add a little life without getting in the way.

When selecting what to put in your work space as decoration, I'd like to make a few suggestions:

1. **INCLUDE ONE OR TWO THINGS THAT REMIND YOU OF PAST SUCCESSES.** In my case, I hung some of my original art pieces that I loved too much to sell. They remind me of my own success and growth in new creative endeavors. I also have stacks of magazines that feature my work or home, since that was one of my loftiest dreams when I started my business. Those stacks remind me of what's possible.

2. **USE A PIECE THAT INSPIRES OR MOTIVATES YOU.** In my office, I take this literally and have a 3' × 4' inspiration board hanging above my desk. I get lost in it sometimes, just staring at the collection of images, color swatches, textiles, and motivating words.

3. **ADD SOMETHING JUST FOR FUN.** I hung my guitar in my office for that very reason. It doesn't have anything to do with my work, but I love that it is visible and accessible whenever I want to play. My dad gave me this guitar shortly after I had Marshall and we had no

expendable income. I never could've bought such a beautiful guitar. It reminds me of my dad, of the humble beginnings my business was born out of, and of the love of music instilled in me by my parents. It makes me smile for all of those reasons and more. I pull it off the wall for intentional practice, but also just to noodle when I'm feeling stuck.

The furniture, arrangement, and organi-zation of the room dictate how well the room functions. It's the finishing touches and personal-ity that dictate how the room *feels*, which can be just as important, especially when you're trying to get some good work done. If a room fosters creativity, ingenuity, focus, calm, clarity, and productivity, your work will typically be easier and more enjoyable. Never underestimate the power of a well-decorated room!

Project: INSTALLING PANELING

WHAT YOU'LL NEED

- Paneling (I used 4' × 8' sheets of faux wood paneling made out of hardboard.)
- Tape measure
- Level
- Pencil
- Screwdriver
- Carpentry square
- Worktable/workbench
- Circular saw or table saw (I used a Dremel Saw-Max, because it's small and easy for me to handle.)
- Jigsaw
- Miter saw
- Drill equipped with large drill bit
- 100-grit sandpaper
- Finish nailer
- 1¼" finishing nails
- Trim for top of paneling
- Caulk
- Primer (If the surface is slick, use an adhesion/bonding primer.)
- Quality paint (I used a satin-finish trim paint.)
- Paint tray and plastic tray liner
- Paint roller
- Microfiber roller cover
- 2½" angled sash brush
- Safety gear—eye and ear protection for when using the saws and a dust mask for sanding

A FEW HELPFUL TIPS

- Handling 4' × 8' panels by yourself can be awkward and difficult, so it's best to do this project when there is an extra set of hands available!
- The paneling can be affixed to the wall with construction adhesive instead of nails, but I wanted future owners of this home to have the option to remove the paneling without damaging the drywall.
- One of the nice things about working with hardboard is that it's thin and easy to cut. You can get away with using smaller handheld saws for this project.

STEPS

1. Measure the walls and plan how the panels will be hung. My ceilings are 9' high and the panels are only 8', so I decided on a two-thirds-height paneling and cut each panel down to 6' using the Saw-Max. This is also a good time to take note of vents, outlets, and anything else that needs to be cut around.

2. Remove outlet and switch covers as well as any vents.

3. Cut the first piece of paneling to the desired height and shape (if it needs to be cut around windows and doorframes). Use the carpentry square and pencil to make your cut lines. Plan to have the "factory edge" along the baseboard, since that will be a perfectly straight cut. If your cut isn't perfectly straight along the top, that can be covered by trim. If there are any switches or outlets to cut around, use a measuring tape to determine the necessary placement of the holes, and draw up a plan with those measurements. Transfer the measurements to the piece of paneling and draw where the holes need to be cut. Double-check those measurements before making any cuts! Drill four holes, large

enough to fit your jigsaw blade, inside the four corners of the marked area. Insert the jigsaw into each hole to cut a straight line along the pencil marks. Sand all cut edges to smooth.

4. Dry fit the panel first, making sure it fits. Rest the paneling along the baseboard and check that it is level. When the panel is fitted and level, nail it into place with a finish nailer.

5. When installing over switches and outlets, turn the power off to the room and loosen the screws holding the outlet or switch to the box. Fit the paneling, pulling the outlet or switch through the hole. Nail the panel in place and screw the outlet or switch back to the box. Longer screws may be required if the paneling is thicker than ¼". When installed this way, the plate will still fit over the outlet or switch and sit flush against the paneling.

6. Repeat steps 3 and 4 with each panel until the room is complete.

7. Top the paneling with a piece of trim, mitering the corners with a miter saw.

8. Caulk the nail holes and seams between the panels and along the baseboards and other trim.

9. Prime the paneling once the caulk is completely dry. Use a quality adhesion primer on faux wood paneling, since it's a smooth, slick surface. If painting the paneling a color other than white, have the primer tinted to that color for better coverage.

10. Paint the paneling and trim with a microfiber roller (meant for smooth surfaces) and a quality 2½" angled sash brush.

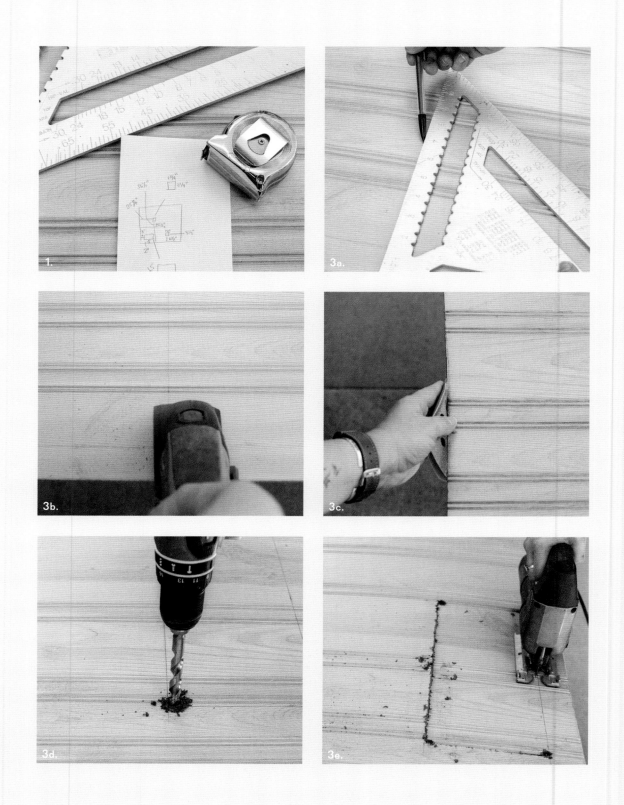

5a.

5b.

The Gift of a *Creative Space*

As I've worked with and mentored entrepreneurs over the years, I've heard the following sentiment repeated multiple times—*I feel selfish taking up an entire room for my creative endeavors/hobbies/projects*. (And let me clarify that creative work isn't just art and music. It can be any kind of hobby or activity.) It can feel luxurious and a little indulgent to dedicate a space to one specific hobby, but it is truly a gift you can give to yourself.

The alternative, which is common, is hobbies and creative pursuits taking over several rooms in the house, which can be disruptive and even frustrating. I know we're not the only family who had to eat off trays for a while because a project had taken over the kitchen table! By claiming a room or even a part of a room, a closet, or what's becoming increasingly more popular, a shed, you're giving your creative work importance. It matters and it deserves dedicated space, even if it's a small space.

Claiming an underutilized space in your home for an activity that nurtures your soul isn't selfish, it's smart. And I would encourage you to create that kind of space not only for yourself, but for the rest of your family members, too. It's a nonverbal way to say, *Your interests are important and we'll make room for them if at all possible*. It could be a place for music, for exercise, for art, for tying flies. It can be whatever it needs to be and wherever it fits.

It's worth taking the time and resources to customize your home to accommodate not only your life and the work that is done from home, but also the activities that make your heart come alive.

CHAPTER VIII

THE REST OF THE
rooms

BATHROOMS, HALLS, LAUNDRY ROOMS, FOYERS & MUDROOMS

DO WHAT YOU CAN, WITH WHAT YOU'VE GOT, WHERE YOU ARE.
—SQUIRE BILLY WIDENER

My conversations with Jeff about decorating are typically pretty comical. I am into decorating. He just wants to make sure my decor doesn't take over his nightstand and that he can actually sit in chairs that I bring into the house (both reasonable requests). When I start digging into the details of decorating a room, his eyes will glaze over, and I can see when he mentally checks out of the conversation. I return the favor by glazing over when he gets into the nitty-gritty of Tolkien's Middle-earth or Civil War history.

So, when I started talking about this chapter dedicated to what I was calling "non-room rooms," I was surprised when he put up some debate. This resulted in a lengthy conversation that neither of us intended about whether a bathroom, mudroom, laundry room, or foyer was a full-fledged room. His argument for was that they are included on a real estate listing and/or have the word "room" included in their description. Fair points. My argument against was that they are pass-through, task-oriented spaces that are generally neglected when it comes to decorating. Not always, but often. I think his argument was better, so this chapter wasn't titled "The Non-Room Rooms," but "The Rest of the Rooms."

When we were prioritizing the projects we wanted to complete in the first couple of years of living in our Minnesota home, the foyer and laundry room didn't even make the list. We really just walk through them, so I felt like our time and money would be better spent elsewhere. After living in the home for several months, though, I realized I walked through those spaces a lot! We all did. Every time we entered the home, it was either through the laundry room or the foyer.

When we had guests over, the foyer was the first thing that welcomed them into our home. It was the first impression. I always found myself moving through those spaces quickly, trying to look past them

This typical beige and boring suburban foyer was transformed with a pale blue-gray paint, bright white trim, wood stairs, and a classic slate floor. Antique furniture and accessories add warmth and character.

Pass-Through
Spaces

These are the hallways, foyers, passages, and stairways. These non-room rooms might claim the number one spot on the neglected list when it comes to decorating. It's understandable, because we don't spend a lot of time in them consecutively. It's only when we really take note of how often we pass through these spaces, as I did, that we recognize they are worth some attention.

Our two-story suburban foyer included a hall that led to the living room, the stairs, and an upstairs hallway to all of the bedrooms. It was a huge pass-through space, which meant there was a lot of potential for customizing, but it also meant it was an overwhelming makeover. I didn't even know how we could paint it without renting scaffolding!

It kicked off with a hopeful DIY project. In an attempt to save money, Jeff and I (well, it was about 99 percent me and 1 percent Jeff) decided we could tackle giving the carpeted steps a makeover ourselves. Solid wood treads were exposed along the railing edge of the steps, and we were hopeful that was an indicator that all of the steps were solid wood. That meant we would just have to rip up the carpet and do some painting and refinishing. Done and done.

Well, as soon as we started removing the carpet, our hopes were dashed. The solid wood butted up against particleboard with raw, rough edges. These couldn't simply be painted. They would have to be removed and replaced. We (I) still felt like it was a doable DIY project for our level of skill, so one day, we started removing

into the rooms where I had invested time and attention. I tried to ignore the thirteen-year-old carpeted stairs that always looked dirty no matter how much I scrubbed and vacuumed them, the laminate cabinets, scuffs on the peachy-cream walls, and the beige tile. But the longer we lived there and the more I passed through those spaces, the higher they climbed on the priority list.

I wanted the first thing to greet us when we walked through the front door or the garage door to be a reflection of us and our preferences. (Well, *my* preferences since Jeff's eyes would glaze over at paint and tile selections.)

one of the particleboard treads. It took about two hours to get one up! It just broke into bits as we tried to pry it up. It was the kind of DIY project that is so slow and difficult that it's painful and deflating. We gave it the good old try and knew we couldn't do this staircase justice. It was time to turn to the pros.

It did make us feel justified in hiring the project out when the professionals said these were some of the hardest treads they'd ever had to remove! Whoever built the house never intended for those to come out again. The contractors were able to install the wood treads in just a couple of days, and the finished result was beautiful and entirely worth it. In addition to hiring out the stairs, we also had the builder-beige 18" × 18" ceramic tiles replaced with Montauk Blue slate, and had all of the walls, trim, and stair railings professionally painted.

I'll take a minute to insert a few thoughts about doing projects yourself (DIY) versus hiring out. For years, I couldn't imagine hiring anything out. As a die-hard DIYer, it seemed like cheating for some reason. When I decided to hire out the painting in our foyer, I felt like I needed to overjustify it to myself, to Jeff, as well as to my blog audience, who have known me as a DIYer for over a decade. I've painted the ceilings, walls, cabinets, and trim in both of my previous houses all by myself. I've tiled my own kitchen backsplash and installed and refinished hardwood floors. Jeff and I even built and installed our own kitchen counters, a custom range hood, and a skylight tube. (Cutting a big hole in the roof was a scary moment!)

But every project is different and every season of life is different. It really is okay, even for the serial DIYer, to budget and pay for outside help. On the flip side, if you've always hired help, it's okay to try to tackle something on your own for the first time. While I love doing projects and we have made about 90 percent of the improvements to our suburban home ourselves, I am glad that I hired out strategically to get a project done quickly and professionally.

While those projects felt like they were more than cosmetic, the projects we had done really were just surface-level changes of the finishes—upgrading the tile, painting the walls and trim, and swapping out carpet for hardwood. Those cosmetic changes made a massive difference in the visual appeal of the space and made it feel more connected to and cohesive with the adjoining rooms. It no longer felt like it was a forgotten part of the house.

FIVE WAYS TO CUSTOMIZE A HALLWAY

1. **PICK A WALL COLOR THAT LOOKS INTEN-TIONAL, AND I SUGGEST A MIDTONE COLOR.** White walls can look really boring in a small hallway. In addition, really light colors and really dark ones show scuffs and marks more noticeably than midtones. Consider the doors and trim when selecting colors. Do you want the doors and the trim to blend with the walls or stand out?

2. **MAKE THE DOORS SPECIAL!** It's amazing what painting a door a color other than white does for a hallway, which is usually a skinny room full of doors! Add trim to the door, custom signs letting people know what's inside

("WC," "Broom Cupboard," "Laundry," etc.), or customize the doors with some upgraded doorknobs.

3. **HANG ART GALLERY–STYLE.** Since a hallway isn't a place where people usually linger, make it a little more interesting by hanging art, family photos, old letters, awards, etc. Make sure the frames don't sit too far out from the wall, since the space might be narrow, and view the wall from every angle. Most halls are viewed from one end or the other, so keep those vantage points in mind.

4. **ADD WALLPAPER OR DETAILED MOLDING TO MAKE THE SPACE LOOK AND FEEL MORE IMPORTANT AND INTERESTING!** Wallpaper can add depth, and molding adds detail (as well as more opportunity for interesting paint treatments). When selecting papers and trim patterns, make sure they are complementing the rooms off the hallway instead of competing with them.

5. **CUSTOMIZE THE LIGHTING.** Hall lights are notoriously nondescript and cheap. Upgrade to something that speaks to your style.

FIVE WAYS TO CUSTOMIZE A FOYER

1. **IF THERE IS ROOM, USE A REAL PIECE OF FURNITURE!** Put a lamp on top to use as a welcoming night-light, a plant to add some life and greenery, and a tray for catching keys.

2. **ADD LARGE HOOKS FOR COATS, DOG LEASHES, AND BAGS, AND SMALL HOOKS FOR KEYS.** Hooks are a great nonverbal cue to hang things up instead of dropping them on the floor! Make sure hooks are secured into studs so they can handle the weight of backpacks.

3. **HANG A PIECE OF ART THAT IS AN INTRODUCTION TO YOUR STYLE AND WHAT CAN BE EXPECTED THROUGH THE REST OF THE HOUSE.** I hung a pair of antique wooden clogs in my foyer as a nod to my love of European antiques as well as my love of using found pieces in unique ways as decor.

4. **ADDRESS CLUTTER WITH SMART SOLUTIONS.** Foyers are magnets for clutter: shoes piled by the door, bags, coats, gloves, boots, mail, etc. Instead of being overwhelmed by the clutter, allowing it to take over, create a system. When everything has a place, mess is easier to control. It won't be perfect, because 100 percent of the people in your home won't follow the system 100 percent of the time, but it'll be better! We use an antique cabinet for backpacks, lunch boxes, hats, and gloves. A small pine chest holds shoes (they can be quickly kicked under or put inside a drawer to keep our dog from carrying them around), leashes, and the dog harness, and a tray sits on top to collect incoming mail.

5. **ADD THOUGHTFUL TOUCHES.** A durable rug can cozy up a space that is generally full of hard surfaces. If you can, add a small chair or bench with a pillow or cushion, too. Soft furnishings make a pass-through space feel more like a real room, and people will appreciate a place to sit when putting on or taking off shoes. Hang a mirror for a last-minute check before leaving the house.

OPPOSITE: A custom-made door, subtle wallpaper, a classic color combination, and a curated collection of antiques make the Nosers' 1970s suburban home feel like it's decades older.

FIVE WAYS TO CUSTOMIZE A STAIRWAY

1. **ADD A RUNNER FOR COMFORT, TEXTURE, COLOR, AND PATTERN.** While hardwood stairs are easiest to keep clean, they can be too slippery for some families. A runner will provide some grip, but it is also a prime place to add style! They are pretty easy to install on your own and can be cleaned or replaced every few years as they wear.

2. **ADD TRIM THAT MIRRORS THE RAILINGS.** Trim can be tricky along a stairway because of the angles, but it is a great way to break up a large expanse of wall. Picture frame molding and board-and-batten are traditional choices for stairways.

3. **ADD A MURAL.** With amazing wallpaper murals on the market, you don't need to be an artist (or hire one) to get this striking look. A mural can add depth and pack a powerful visual punch. (You can find a mural tutorial in chapter V.)

4. **CHANGE OUT THE RAILINGS OR SPINDLES.** When we started working on our stairs, I assumed removing the spindles and railings would be a nightmare, but they came out by simply backing out a few screws. I liked the style of our spindles, but it would've been relatively easy to change them out to something different.

5. **BRING OUT THE PAINT.** If you do have wooden stairs that are worn or made of low-grade wood, paint is an easy and inexpensive way to make them look fresh. Paint the risers and treads in contrasting colors to make the steps easier to see and more interesting to the eye.

The Half Bathroom: Creating a Jewel Box

If you're scared of color, wallpaper, patterns, or any decorating choices that are too one way or another, a half bathroom is a perfect place to dip your toe into other styles and color palettes. It's typically a tiny room that is used only out of requirement and will always (hopefully) have a door to close it off from other parts of the home, so have fun with it!

When putting together a design for a half

bathroom, think about it as a little jewel box. When the door is opened, it offers a delightful surprise that is an extension of, but maybe a slight departure from, the rest of the house. Here are a few ways to do that:

- Pick a color that is a more extreme version of what you love. If you gravitate toward blues, try a deep navy or a bright royal. If you like pinks, try a bold fuchsia or rich raspberry. Just push it a little bit further than you normally would.
- If you are considering wallpaper, try a busy pattern that would overwhelm the eye in a larger room. It's also a great place to use murals to add depth or graphic patterns like plaids and dots.
- If going bold with paint and paper doesn't feel like your style, try making a statement with repetition. Hang a collection of small items like vintage hand mirrors, combs, razors, or shaving brushes. When grouped together, the effect can be striking.
- A chunky molding can also make a small room feel special. Just because the room is small doesn't mean the details need to be.
- Make the sink special! Since it's the only piece of "furniture" in the room other than the great throne, treat it thoughtfully. Fit a sink into a small dresser, chest, or table to add some warmth through wood tones. Add a sink skirt to soften a pedestal sink and provide a little hidden storage for extra toilet paper and cleaning supplies.

If there is one room to try out nutty ideas, push the limits, and get a little playful, this is it.

Assignment:
GENTLY PUSH THE LIMITS

Put together a mood board (virtual or in real life) for your powder room, making choices that are just outside of your comfort zone. Revisit that mood board over a period of a few weeks. Are you warming up to it? Are you excited about testing out some of those ideas? If so, go for it as soon as time, budget, and energy allow. If it feels a little too far outside of your comfort zone, what elements can you pull back on? You can always try one idea at a time, live with it for a while, and see if you want to move forward with your original plan or do some fine-tuning.

This salvaged antique sink ended up costing less than purchasing a new vanity! It adds character and style to the upstairs bathroom in the Nosers' home.

A colorful antique rug provides a visual pop in
this classic and serene en suite bathroom.

Suburban *En Suite Bathroom* Makeover

When I first studied the pictures of what would be our bathroom in our potential new house, I was thrilled! In almost twenty years of marriage, Jeff and I had always shared a sink and had a shower-bath combo. This bathroom was big, had tons of storage in the vanity, two sinks, a shower, and, best of all, a deep soaking jetted tub. This bathroom would be the best bathroom we'd ever had.

I couldn't help but see the untapped potential in it. While it was big and had all of the right amenities, it had been finished primarily with low-end, builder-grade materials. The faucets, the lights, the large plate mirror, the plastic shower "phone booth" insert, and the 18" × 18" beige ceramic tile were all cheap, basic finishes. They didn't seem to match the luxurious layout and generous size.

Renovating the bathroom would be a major project, even though almost all of the changes I had in mind would be strictly cosmetic. It ended up taking three years of planning and saving before we were finally ready to start the demolition.

I decided to act as my own designer and project manager, and I would work with specialized tradespeople for the tiling, plumbing, and electrical work. In order to save some money, I would do the painting and trim and coordinate the work. We'd done a few bathroom makeovers before, so I had a little bit of experience under my belt and was able to work with excellent professionals who guided me through uncharted

territory, like letting me know that I needed a permit for the plumbing change I wanted to make in the shower.

It was a hybrid solution that ended up saving us money but didn't put the project entirely on our shoulders. We'd done plumbing, tile, and basic electrical work, but, given that this was a second-floor bathroom, everything had to be done 100 percent right. This bathroom makeover was also like a line of dominoes. You couldn't redo the shower without redoing the floor and the tub surround. Then the vanity counter wouldn't match, and if we were replacing that, then we should get the wall behind it right, etc. This was a project that needed to be worked on as a whole.

As I do with most projects, I took a high-low

approach. I splurged where it really counted and saved where I could. One example of that was the tile I selected for the tub surround, shower, and vanity wall. I originally wanted 3" × 6" subway tiles and priced it out. Having installed subway tile in our previous bathroom, I knew it was labor intensive, therefore increasing the cost. The tiles alone were almost twice the expense of 6" × 12" tiles. After searching for some inspiration pictures, I was able to see that the 6" × 12" tiles arranged in a staggered subway pattern would give me the same look for about half the cost.

I splurged on the marble, the shower and bath faucets, and the clear glass door. I saved by reusing the tub, buying the mirrors on sale,

purchasing the sinks from a discount store, and painting the vanity myself with paint I already had. I also purchased most of the towels from a discount store, and the shelf in the niche over the tub was a consignment store find.

It took about a month of having a toilet sitting in our bedroom along with the contents of the vanity cabinets and some of the linen closet, but we made it through! The finishes of the bathroom now match the size and features. It feels special, luxurious, and spa-like. In addition, we gained almost three square feet of space in the shower without having to move any walls.

PROJECT MANAGEMENT TIPS

If the renovation of a bathroom or kitchen is in your future and you're considering managing the project on your own, here are a few things I've learned from my own experiences:

- If you're unsure of your design choices from a practical or technical standpoint, run them by the specialists you are hiring. I was able to have my plumber take a look at the shower fixtures so they would know what was required for the install.
- It will be up to you to order all of the materials, and you will be making a million little decisions about bull-nosed edges and mitered corners, how wide the shower door should be and which way it will swing. You can think you have all of the decisions made, and there will still be more that pop up as the project progresses. Be prepared for that and don't feel pressured to make a decision you're unsure about.
- Hire skilled specialists who understand your vision for the space and aren't trying to talk you into something that doesn't work with that vision. It's a bonus if they make suggestions that improve the look and make it even better!
- It's also important to hire people who are thorough and detail oriented and who care about making sure the job is done right and to your specifications. Our tile installer helped us with planning out the order of the renovation, tipped us off to when we needed to call an electrician to get some wires moved, helped us hang the vanity mirrors, and even pointed out a spot where our roof was leaking. All of these things were above and beyond laying tile and grouting. In addition to being meticulous, he wanted to make sure the entire project was done right.
- Be realistic about your comfort level with managing a renovation. Bathrooms, kitchens, additions, etc. are expensive, messy, and disruptive and are semipermanent changes to your home that you hope will look good for many years. We all want to save money on home projects, but there are times when it's best to hire a professional. Know when that time is!

Our *Laundry* Room/Mudroom

Another feature of our new home that excited me was the laundry room/mudroom. We didn't have either in our previous home. The front door opened right onto the living room, so we turned an old kitchen, which was two rooms away from the front door, into an office/mudroom. It was a place to land, store backpacks, hang coats, etc. Our laundry room was down an open flight of steps into a 1940s basement with a low-hanging ceiling and cobwebbed cinderblock walls. Being able to do my laundry aboveground was a welcome change! And I was thrilled to have a place to kick off snowy boots before going farther into the house.

This laundry room/mudroom combo was like the rest of the rooms in our house—beige and dingy cream, builder basic. At first, I didn't pay too much attention to it, because it's a mudroom. It doesn't have to be pretty. As long as the washer and dryer are running and the pile of shoes is under control, this room is serving its purpose. But, as with the foyer, we quickly realized we were in and out of this room a lot. It's the first thing we saw when we came home, and it didn't really feel like home. It felt like the little room we passed through before we were officially home. I wanted to change that.

As I studied the room, I knew it just needed

OPPOSITE: Cheap laminate cabinets were backed with beadboard and painted to give this laundry room a cottage look on a budget. Corbels and a sink skirt were added to lend even more charm.

some personality and a lot of paint! It didn't need a full overhaul, but just cosmetic changes that I could easily do myself. While Jeff was on a hiking trip the summer after we moved in, I tackled it!

I started out by installing thin beadboard along all of the walls. Instead of going with the traditional vertical beadboard, I installed it horizontally up to about 7' and vertically the remaining 2'. I had seen similar tongue-and-groove walls in a beautiful bed-and-breakfast online and had wanted to emulate that look for a long time. The laundry room/mudroom was the perfect place to do it. I also removed the doors from the melamine cabinets. The flat fronts were boring and a little too 1980s for the look I was going for. Open cabinetry is a fun way to display some more of my ironstone collection, and it holds me accountable when it comes to keeping things tidy. If it's out in the open, I'm going to keep it neat!

The room needed some color, so I painted the cabinets with the same custom-mixed grassy green I used on my island and butler's pantry and backed the open shelving with beadboard as well. The walls got a couple of coats of bright white paint to make the space feel fresh. An antique piece of toweling was repurposed as a sink skirt to hide cleaning supplies. As I did with all of the interior doors in the house, I painted the doors a midtone gray, which sets them apart from the white walls and trim.

This makeover ended up being one of the most dramatic in our entire house. It's a testament to how paint, beadboard, and good old-fashioned hard work can completely transform a room.

FORM AND FUNCTION

Jeff and I often have the form versus function debate. He cares more about function and not so much about how it looks. (Although, I think he's coming around a little bit.) I care more about form but will argue until the sun goes down that things and spaces can be both. Just because it's functional does not mean it has to be unsightly. Just look at all of the stylish toilets and beautiful appliances available in the world today. There is a myriad of choices when it comes to all basic household needs. If you have a choice, choose something that works with your style. I would argue that you will take better care of the things you use every day, the practical, basic things, if you love the way they look.

Here are some ways to make practical things beautiful in laundry rooms and mudrooms:

- If there is room, use a freestanding piece of furniture. Furniture, whether painted or wood, adds a hominess to a space that's typically filled with built-in closets and cabinets. Select a piece of furniture that will be a good home for the stuff you need to store—shoes, laundry soap, cleaning supplies, etc.

- Pick a hard-wearing, beautiful rug. It'll add color and pattern, prevent slipping when the floor is wet, and give a spot for wiping wet shoes and paws. Antique or vintage wool rugs are my favorite for this purpose. Wool is so durable and forgiving when it comes to dirt, pets, water, etc. They will last your entire life and beyond.

- Select hooks that can handle the heavy weight of multiple coats, purses, or backpacks, and reinforce your style. I love looking for antique and vintage hooks sold in lots that are unique.

- Replace a plastic utility sink with something with more personality. Salvaged sinks can be found on local marketplaces or in consignment shops, thrift stores, and architectural salvage stores.

- Put cleaners, soaps, dryer balls, clothespins, etc. into pretty containers like jars, baskets, and wooden bowls.

- Hang art in the room! In our laundry/mudroom, I hung antique signs to add a little bit of character along with an antique drying rack and a couple of original paintings.

ER

ods Co.

Minneapolis: 501-503-505-507 NICOLLET AVENUE,
New York: 454 BROOME STREET,
Manchester, Paris, Chemnitz,
17 Nicholas St. 39 Rue De L'Echiquier. 33 Theatre Strasse.

5 1-2 Yards=1 Rod.   320 Rods=1 Mile.

10 Decimetres=1 Metre.

7   8   9   10   11   12

CHAPTER IX

CUSTOM *furnishings*

fur·nish·ing
/ˈfərniSHiNG/
noun
plural noun: furnishings
furniture, fittings, and other decorative accessories,
such as curtains and carpets, for a house or room

IF I HAD TO CHOOSE BETWEEN CLOTHES AND FURNITURE, I'D CHOOSE FURNITURE.
—JULIANNE MOORE

There is something about furniture—specifically old furniture that is sturdy and well built, that has stood the test of time, that has hidden treasures like dovetail joints, hand-chiseled pocket holes and maker's marks—that draws me in. It doesn't matter what is on my shopping list, if I see a beautiful piece of furniture, I can't help but stop and admire it. This is a very impractical infatuation, by the way, because you can fit only so much furniture in your home (and garage) and I will have to drive a minivan for the rest of my life so that I can always fit a piece of found furniture in my vehicle to take it home.

This love of furniture was probably born out of hours of playing with and rearranging hand-painted Bavarian dollhouse furniture as a child. This love was stoked when I bought and refinished a ten-dollar vintage dresser as a newlywed. My love of furniture grew to such an extent that it naturally became a significant part of my business.

For more than ten years, I have been buying and selling furniture, fixing it up along the way, all the while making tutorials and writing blog posts, teaching others how to save their own furniture finds. I have refinished, rebuilt, repainted, reupholstered, and repurposed hundreds and hundreds of pieces. For years, my home was a temporary stop for neglected furniture. I would fix it up, love on it, and ready it for a new home. I would then send it off to be loved by someone else, leaving holes in my own home that were soon filled with new pieces that needed attention.

Just as I do with houses, I also have lost-dog syndrome for furniture.

As much as I love decorating in general, it's my love of furniture that drives most of my decorating decisions.

One of my dear friends and fellow furniture lovers, Barb Blair, wrote a book entitled *Furniture Makes the Room*, and I believe that sentiment to be 100 percent true. That statement doesn't prescribe a specific formula for what the furniture has to be, but simply that the furniture put in a room can make or break it. It can be coordinated, mismatched, high-end, thrifted, museum quality, custom-made, hand-me-down, heirloom, curbside found, brand-new, antique, vintage, and everything in between.

Bottom line—the furniture matters.

It's not just a place to sit or sleep or eat. It's not just a way to fill a space.

Furniture defines the purpose of a room, contributes to the character of a room, and acts as the anchor for everything else. In several of the rooms featured in this book, the room itself is pretty simple. It's the furniture that makes it unique and feel like home to the family who lives there. So be intentional about the furniture you bring into your home and show some love to the pieces you currently have.

Prepping a Piece of
Furniture to Paint

If you have a piece of furniture that is sturdy and in good, usable condition, but it's dated, has some cosmetic damage, or simply doesn't work with your vision for the room, paint is the easiest way to give it an entirely new look. As much as I love paint, I don't think every piece should be painted, but it's a good answer for a lot of decorating dilemmas that involve furniture.

We'll talk about making the decision to paint a piece later in this chapter, but for now, let's assume you've decided to paint a piece and you want to know how to do it properly. A good paint job starts with good prep work. I know, I know; prep work isn't fun. Who wants to spend their time sanding? You do. You really do, even if you don't.

I will defend sanding to my dying breath, because I've learned from experience that a little bit of sanding can make a substantial difference in the quality of the final finish. I've also learned that it doesn't have to be a long, laborious process that completely removes the existing finish on the piece you're painting, but just five minutes with an orbital sander to take off the shine.

This vintage dresser, purchased for $50, got a stunning makeover with black milk paint and a hemp oil finish.

There are other advantages to sanding beyond just giving the surface tooth. It's also a get-to-know-you time with your piece. I always run my hand over the piece as I'm sanding it. Are there places where the finish has been eaten away? Are there drips or brushstrokes from previous paint jobs or finish applications? Is there loose or chipping veneer? Are there places that need to be repaired? Sticky drawers that need to be waxed or sanded? While you're sanding, you can answer all of these questions and address them prior to applying a fresh coat of paint.

1. **REMOVE HARDWARE** (this includes handles, pulls, casters, key escutcheons, etc.). If a piece of hardware cannot be removed, mask it off with painter's tape or coat it in petroleum jelly to resist the paint.

2. **SAND.** As you read in my essay defending sanding, I am pretty insistent on this step! Use 80- to 150-grit sandpaper to rough up the surface. (If you're brand new to sandpaper, visit the sandpaper primer on page 219 for all the gritty details.) This isn't about removing the finish, but just taking the shine off and creating an even surface to accept the first layer of primer or paint. Wear a mask when sanding and test the piece before sanding if there are concerns about lead paint.

3. **REPAIR.** This is the time to make any repairs that the piece may require. If a drawer doesn't open and close easily, try rubbing it with candle wax or sanding the area that is sticking to remove some of the wood. If a joint is loose, it may require some wood glue and clamps to tighten it up or even a carefully placed screw.

    Now you're ready to paint.

Cleaning Stinky Pieces of *Furniture*

When it comes to refinishing furniture, this is the question I'm asked the most! "How do I remove _____ smell from a piece of furniture?"

I always suggest giving a piece the "sniff test" before you buy it. This comes from years of experience of buying pieces without sticking my face down in the cushion or in the drawers and regretting it later. Severe smoke and pet smells will be almost impossible to completely remove.

SANDPAPER PRIMER

If you don't care to know anything else about sandpaper, know this—the lower the number, the rougher the paper.

For those who are a bit more inquisitive, here are common grits of sandpaper and their uses:

40–80: These are heavy grit and rough, which means they are good for stripping (removing finishes or paint). You would also use these grits for removing material from wood to make it fit in a specific space, like a drawer or door that's sticking in its recess.

80–120: These are good all-purpose grits that are useful when it comes to light sanding, rough finishing, smoothing out imperfections in a surface or finish, or for distressing paint and finishes.

120–220: These fine papers can be used in the same situations as the 80–120 category, but the finish will be softer and smoother.

220+: This is superfine sandpaper that's meant for getting a baby-smooth finish. It's also used between coats of paint or finish to eliminate application marks.

The best way to use sandpaper is in sequence from rough to smooth. If you're refinishing a tabletop, for example, start with 40- to 80-grit paper to remove any existing finish. Once the finish is stripped, move to 100–120 to smooth the surface of the wood. Switch to 180–220 to make the surface even smoother before applying a new finish. Use 220 or higher between coats of finish to smooth application marks.

You can minimize them, but they will always be noticeable.

Most pieces, though, will just be a little musty and dusty. They'll have a few cobwebs on the bottom and just need to be refreshed. Here are the steps I'll go through to get a piece looking and smelling its best:

1. **RUN A VACUUM OVER THE ENTIRE PIECE.** Pull out the drawers and vacuum those, the cavities, the underside, the back, everything. This will get rid of any cobwebs and surface-level dust and dirt. For most pieces, a good vacuum and a few lavender sachets in the drawers will do the trick.

2. **IF THE DRAWERS STILL SMELL TOO MUSTY TO USE** (particularly for table linens or clothes), put a charcoal briquette or a cup of ground coffee inside the drawers for a few days. You can also let the drawers air out on a breezy, sunny day.

3. **IF THE PIECE IS STILL STINKY, WASH IT.** Use a mild dish soap (or a soap meant for wood, like Murphy Oil Soap) and wash it with a bucket of warm soapy water and a scrub brush. I used this trick on some pieces hauled out of barns that smelled very farmy and they cleaned up great. It's okay to get the wood wet, just put it outside on a sunny day to dry. Also, make sure it's completely dry before you paint or finish it.

4. **IF SOAP AND WATER DOESN'T DO THE TRICK, CLEAN IT WITH A WATER AND VINEGAR MIXTURE.** Vinegar is a natural cleaner and deodorizer (even though it stinks!). Wipe it down and let it dry.

5. **IF THE SMELL IS ABSOLUTELY STUBBORN AND YOU'RE ABOUT READY TO BURN THE PIECE,** try one last thing! Prime the entire piece, inside and out, with an odor-blocking primer. This will seal in strong smells and make the piece usable. You can then paint it to finish it off.

Which Paint Is the Right Paint?

There is a vast array of paints available on the market today. As a paint enthusiast, I have tried many of them. I don't think there is one be-all and end-all paint for every scenario, so I have a large paint shelf with many different brands and varieties of paint to use. It is my go-to option when it comes to customizing just about anything, so it's a topic worth exploring in depth. To help you sift through the decision of which paint to use when, here are the paints I use along with their pros and cons.

MILK PAINT

PROS

- It is one of the oldest forms of paint, so it has passed the test of time.
- It is thin, so it is forgiving for sloppy painters and it's easy to fix drips. You can easily apply multiple, thin coats for a beautiful finish and depth of color.

- It distresses in a very authentic way, so if you like the distressed look, milk paint is the paint to reach for.
- It is quick drying, so most pieces can be completed in a day.
- Because it doesn't have the modern-day additives that make paint adhere to smooth surfaces, it will resist certain finishes, creating an authentic "chippy" look.

- It has a depth of color and beautiful color variations due to the way it's pigmented.
- It is the absolute best paint I know of for raw wood and porous surfaces, because it soaks in like a stain, but looks like a paint. This means it will never chip or wear away. There are pieces of furniture that are over one hundred years old with the original milk paint still on them. That is durability!

Not only was this child's landscape dresser painted with milk paint, but so was the antique mirror frame. The interior backing was painted with a custom-mixed color to look like a vintage chalkboard.

- In powdered form, it has an indefinite shelf life, so this paint can be used once a decade and it will still be there waiting for you to use on your next project.

CONS

- It comes in powdered form and needs to be mixed with water. It may take some practice to get used to the consistency you want for your project. The texture is so different from "modern" paints that it freaks some people out!

- When using it over an existing finish, it can be unpredictable. Sometimes it will chip a lot, sometimes a little, sometimes not at all.

- For most pieces, it needs some kind of protective topcoat (oil, poly, wax, water-based poly, etc.). I have left milk paint unfinished and it is beautiful in pale blues, grays, and greens, but the piece will absorb oils and stains much easier.

WHEN I USE IT

- I love milk paint for vintage and antique furniture, but it can be used for cabinetry, walls, floors (it's especially perfect for raw wood floors), fabric, masonry, and more.

TIPS FOR SUCCESS WITH MILK PAINT

- It is a unique paint, so I always suggest testing it out on something small or a free or thrifted piece, so you get a feel for how the paint flows off the brush and reacts to the surface you're painting. Experience is the best teacher when it comes to any paint, but this is doubly true with milk paint.

- Your paint mix will be thin and should run off a stir stick in a string (as opposed to a ribbon as is typical with most other paints).

- Mix only what you need. Milk paint will last for a few days once it's mixed with water and then it has to be disposed of.

- Because of the color variation, always apply milk paint in a complete coat. Touch-ups can result in uneven color.

ACRYLIC PAINT

PROS

- It flows off a brush beautifully and has great body. It's just the right amount of thickness to give good coverage without getting gloppy.

- It's durable with or without a topcoat.

- It can generally be used without primer, although I would suggest a primer for slick surfaces like laminate.

- It looks great rolled, sprayed, or brushed, and it distresses well when it's in a matte or flat finish.

- Most formulas have no VOCs and are almost odorless.

- It's fast drying and can be recoated within about an hour.

CONS

- Most readily available acrylic paint is "craft paint," which comes in tiny bottles. Acrylic is becoming more widely available for furniture and home projects, though.

- Quality acrylic is on the pricey side. I know ninety-nine cents per bottle makes it seem cheap, but if you make a gallon out of that, it's expensive.

WHEN I USE IT

- I use it mostly for decorative painting, because it has a nice body, but I also like it for furniture. It does well on finished and raw wood, painted surfaces, metal, fabric, and more.

TIPS FOR SUCCESS WITH ACRYLICS

- Acrylic paint can dry very fast! If you need additional working time, add an extender that will keep the paint workable for longer.
- Make sure that the surface you're painting is free from oils or wax, which acrylic paint can resist.

CHALK-CLAY AND CHALK-TYPE PAINT

PROS

- It is designed to have fantastic adhesive qualities, so it will stick to almost anything without sanding, prep, or primer.
- The paint is thick, so it gives good coverage and can be used to create interesting textures.
- It's low odor and fast drying.
- It's a hard-wearing, durable paint.
- A little goes a long way. It varies based on the brand, but in most cases, one quart will cover a lot of square footage.

- It looks good rolled, sprayed, or brushed, and it also distresses well.

CONS

- Because the paint is thick and "grippy," the brush can drag when you need to apply more than one coat.

WHEN I USE IT

- I like to use it on tricky surfaces like metal, laminate, pieces with glossy paint, etc. or when I want a quick, opaque finish. I've also learned it makes a great primer for milk paint!

This clean-lined vintage dresser was given a feminine makeover with a soft robin's-egg blue paint, hand-painted swirls, and glass knobs.

When she wakes she will move mountains

TIPS FOR SUCCESS WITH CHALK-TYPE PAINTS

- Once the piece is dry, sand the surface with fine sandpaper (220 grit) to achieve a buttery-smooth finish.
- While prep work isn't required, it's always a good idea to give your piece a light sanding before you paint, just to get your hands on it and identify any areas that might be problematic when painting (water rings, loose joints or veneer, etc.).

LATEX PAINT

PROS

- Because latex paint is sold as a base paint and pigments are added in the store, it's readily available in any color imaginable.
- It's relatively inexpensive, especially for small projects. You can get test pots of latex paint for about five dollars, and those can be used on small projects.
- It has a beautiful, consistent finish when sprayed.
- It's durable once it's cured (about thirty days).

CONS

- You have to prep, sand, and prime a piece before using latex.
- It doesn't distress very well, but sort of rolls or peels off.
- It can be unforgiving with brushstrokes and roller marks. A high-quality latex, a good brush, and skilled application can offset that, but it's definitely not a paint you can be sloppy with.
- It can mar or scratch easily until it's fully cured, especially on a piece of furniture.

WHEN I USE IT

- I use it primarily for walls and ceilings. I used to use it on furniture, but I like other paints so much better that I haven't for years. I still wouldn't discount it altogether, though!

TIPS FOR SUCCESS WITH LATEX

- When using it on furniture, always prime with a high-quality bonding primer for a longer-lasting finish. Good finishes are more about the base coat than the finish coat!
- If possible, spray the finish onto furniture and cabinets to eliminate brushstrokes and roller marks.

- If the paint is on the thick side, mix in an additive like Floetrol to minimize brushstrokes and roller marks.

OIL PAINT

- It is very durable. You can scrub it, bang it, scratch it, and scrape it, and it will hold up very well.
- It has a long "open time," meaning you can brush over it and fix drips.
- It is self-leveling, so you can get a nice, smooth finish.
- I think it's the most beautiful paint in a glossy finish. It seems to shine like no other paint!
- It does not require a topcoat.

CONS

- It's stinky.
- It takes a long time to dry—several hours to days depending on the number of coats.
- It is typically cleaned up with solvents, which are also stinky. (You can clean up oil paints with oil-based soaps to reduce exposure to solvents.)
- Colors can yellow over time, which can be an issue with whites.

WHEN I USE IT

- I used it on the kitchen cabinets in my Pennsylvania home because of its durability, and, despite the cons, it was a great option. It's also

a good option for trim. Most oil-based home paint has been replaced with waterborne oils and enamels.
- I also think it's a fantastic paint for exterior doors.

TIPS FOR SUCCESS WITH OILS

- Preparedness is key, since the dry time is longer and special cleanup is required. Make sure you have the time and the materials to complete your project.
- To remove oil paint from clothing or hands, use Murphy Oil Soap or an olive oil–based soap. Baby oil also works well to remove paint from your hands.

WATERBORNE ENAMEL

PROS

- It is also very durable and dries to a hard finish.
- It is typically thin and self-leveling, resulting in a smooth, mark-free finish even when applied with a brush or roller.
- It goes through a paint sprayer well for a perfectly smooth, professional finish when painting furniture or cabinetry.
- Because it's water based, it's nonyellowing and easy to clean up.
- It's relatively fast drying and durable during the thirty-day cure time.
- Because it is a hard-drying finish, it doesn't require an extra topcoat.

CONS

- It's a little stinkier than your typical latex, but that does depend on the brand.
- Since it is normally on the thin side of the paint spectrum, it is prone to dripping and can require more coats.
- Quality waterborne enamels can be pretty pricey but are definitely worth it.

WHEN I USE IT

- I used this on the cabinets, built-ins, and trim in my current home. I also used it on my painted studio floors.

TIPS FOR SUCCESS WITH ENAMEL PAINTS

- Since the paint is thinner, it has a tendency to drip. Apply it in thin coats to prevent dripping, and always look back over your work before it dries to fix any drips.
- Use a microfiber roller designed for trim to prevent roller marks.

Selecting the *Right* Finish

I think finishes are one of the most misunderstood products when it comes to protecting painted or refinished furniture, so let's talk about the different groups of finishes on the market. In all of the furniture painting and refinishing workshops I've taught over the years, I divide finishes into three groups—penetrating, buildable, and hybrid. Understanding how each finish functions will help you make a better choice about the one that will be best for your project.

PENETRATING FINISHES: HEMP OIL, TUNG OIL, AND LINSEED OIL

These are finishes that absorb into a surface like a lotion would on our skin. It soaks into the grain of the wood or the pores of the paint in order to make a durable finish that won't chip or flake away over time. Penetrating finishes tend to have a slower dry and cure time, but they look soft and natural, which is very fitting for wood or antique pieces. They are also easy to repair over the years. You can just give the finish a light sanding with fine sandpaper or steel wool and rub in more oil.

These finishes should be applied in a very thin coat, and excess wiped away with a lint-free cloth. (I like to use a microfiber cloth.) Oils need to be applied over a porous surface like raw or stained wood or a flat-finish paint. If you apply an oil over a satin, semigloss, or gloss paint, it will just sit on top, making a sticky mess.

BUILDABLE FINISHES: POLYURETHANE, WATER-BASED POLY, AND VARNISH

These are finishes that can be applied in layers and built up to increase durability and shine. They are best applied with a sprayer or a high-quality brush. Buildable finishes are harder to apply, because they tend to show brush and roller marks, drips, etc. They do cure harder than penetrating finishes, though, so they are a good option when durability is key.

Keep in mind that while these finishes are hard wearing, they are also more difficult to repair. A significant scratch, gouge, or watermark will typically mean that the entire surface needs to be refinished. You cannot easily "spot repair" pieces with a buildable finish.

HYBRID FINISHES: WAXES

Waxes are the best of both worlds in that they penetrate the surface, but can also be built up in layers. This is also true of some oils. Waxes are time-consuming to apply, but they can provide a rich, buttery finish that is absolutely beautiful. Another advantage to wax is the variation you can get in sheen from just one product. It can be very matte, or you can create a glossy luster by adding more layers and finishing with an electric buffer (or a felt buffing pad added to an orbital sander).

These finishes are easier to repair when damaged, like the penetrating finishes, but they can be higher maintenance. A waxed surface should be waxed and buffed every few years and perhaps more often depending on use.

RIGHT: A hemp oil finish soaks into an old, raw tabletop, hydrating the wood and adding protection.
BELOW LEFT: A collection of old brushes hangs on the studio wall, ready to be used.
BELOW RIGHT: A brown-tinted wax stains and protects a new pine tabletop.

The last thing I want to note about finishes is that if you don't need one, don't use one! It's energy and expense you don't need to expend when working with certain paints. If you're using a quality latex, enamel, acrylic, or oil paint in satin, semigloss, or gloss, you do not need to add a finish. Those paints will be durable enough on their own.

Bespoke Paint

Did you know that you can customize paint colors? There are typically thousands of colors in a paint deck to choose from, but color is so complex that you still might not find just the perfect shade. In that case, you have some options:

- One brand can match colors from another brand. This is a handy thing to know if you have a particular brand you love but find yourself drawn to a color created by another brand. The store can simply match the color for you. This can take a little bit of tweaking, so make sure the mixer is patient and willing to work on the mix until you're happy with the match.
- In addition to matching other paint chips, paint stores can match anything that has a consistent color that is larger than a quarter. I've had paints mixed to match fabrics, custom colors that I've mixed at home using pigments, and even a book cover. With this option, color possibilities truly are endless.
- You can also tweak the colors on the paint chips. This is particularly handy when it comes to mixing whites and very pale colors. It can be difficult to decipher the undertone of a

particular white, but you will know the undertone if your starting point is a darker color. Request to have the color mixed at 75 percent, 50 percent, or even 25 percent and the result will be a paler version of the color on the paint chip. You can also ask for the color to be mixed at 125 percent or 150 percent to make it darker and more intense.

- Don't be afraid to mix colors yourself! Start with small batches and always mix paints that are the same sheen (gloss, matte, satin, etc.) and brand, but you can certainly create your own colors. This is a great option when you're using paints that come premixed in set color palettes.

When customizing a color at the paint store, know that it's going to take a little longer than using a standard formula, so go to the store when it's slow. Also, make sure the mixer takes the time to dry the color and confirm that you're happy with it before you make the purchase. Custom colors are generally nonrefundable, so don't settle! If you do get home and the color isn't working, you can take it back to the store to have them add more pigments to adjust the color.

To Paint or
Not to Paint. . .

That is the question I'm asked most frequently when it comes to painting a piece of furniture. "Should I paint it?" Typically, when someone is asking that question, they want to paint it and they just need someone to give them a nudge. While I love painting furniture, I always suggest waiting until you're 100 percent in the paint camp. It's always easier to paint something than to unpaint it!

I wouldn't suggest painting antiques (and we're talking well over one hundred years old) if they are:

IN PRISTINE CONDITION,

RARE AND VALUABLE,

WEARING THEIR ORIGINAL PAINT OR
    FINISH, OR

HAVE A PATINA THAT WILL BE LOST IF
    PAINTED.

There is a lot of resistance from certain people when it comes to painting anything old or solid wood at all, but those really are the best candidates to paint. They can always be repainted, refinished, or stripped down the road. And they are high-quality enough to be worth the time to paint. Pieces that are made of particleboard and plastics might be worth painting in a pinch but aren't going to last very long. A wood piece can function for generations.

Reproduction pieces that were mass-produced in the early to mid-1900s are not particularly valuable unless they have a notable maker's mark and are in original condition. Those are mostly machine-made pieces that will not be devalued if they are painted. I will paint earlier pieces from the 1800s if they have been refinished before or are in poor condition. There are many cases where these pieces are wearing a thick coat of yellowing polyurethane that was applied in the past fifty years or so and detracts from the beauty of the old wood instead of adds to it.

In the end, it's your piece of furniture! It belongs to you, and if you want to paint it, paint it. If you don't, don't. Customizing furniture to suit your style and needs doesn't require permission from people who don't own or use the piece in question.

This antique pine hutch has a beautiful patina that is just too pretty to paint.

Project: PAINTING A PIECE OF FURNITURE

Think of this project as a "Choose Your Happy Ending" for a particular piece. We've talked about preparing a piece and have compared different paint and finish options. Now it's time to pick what combination is best for your project. There are some guidelines, but there really isn't a right or wrong when it comes to furniture painting. Testing out different combinations is a part of the discovery process and learning what will help you achieve the look that is uniquely you.

   Always test out your ideas on one drawer or the back side of a piece to make sure you're happy with the look. That will save you a lot of time and heartache!

WHAT YOU'LL NEED

- Piece of furniture to paint (It can be new or used, painted, finished, or raw wood. While you can paint laminate, pressboard, etc., I would suggest sticking to a solid wood piece when you're first starting out.)
- Sandpaper in a variety of grits (See the Sandpaper Primer on page 219.)
- Orbital or palm sander (optional)
- 2½" angled sash brush
- Paint roller and roller cover or paint sprayer (optional)
- Paint (Review the pros and cons of different kinds of paint to select the one that is best for your project.)
- Primer and a finish (Optional, depending on the kind of paint you're using. I'll be using milk paint for my project, so I don't need a primer, but I do need a finish.)
- Drop cloth
- Safety gear—dust mask for sanding

A FEW HELPFUL TIPS

- If this is your first time painting a piece of furniture, paint one that isn't precious to you or anyone else. This should be a no-pressure experience, and painting a valuable family heirloom will not be no-pressure.
- Almost all painted furniture goes through an "ugly stage." It will look streaky and horrible when you're halfway through the project, but just keep going until the end. Sometimes it's the very final coat that brings it all together.

STEPS

1. Prep the piece of furniture following the steps on pages 216–218.

2. If using a primer, apply it with a brush, roller, or sprayer. I have grown to love applying paint with simply a brush. A quality brush and paint will leave very few (if any) brushstrokes and will allow you to get into all of the nooks and crannies of a piece. A roller or sprayer is nice if you're working on several pieces or ones that are very large or intricate (like an entire dining set).

3. Apply the paint with a brush, roller, or sprayer. Expect to apply two coats of paint for most colors, allowing for dry time between the two coats.

4. Apply desired finish, if necessary. Reference pages 220–229 to see which paints require a finish. My two favorite finishes for furniture are hemp oil (for dark and saturated colors and raw or stained wood) and a clear water-based Polycrylic (for whites and lighter colors for a more durable finish).

5. Most paints and finishes require thirty days to fully cure. You can use some pieces (like those painted in milk and chalk or clay paints) the same day. Pieces painted in latex should be allowed to cure for a few days prior to moving them or putting them back into daily use.

Customizing a New, *Store-Bought* Piece of *Furniture*

There are times when a new piece of furniture is more functional than a thrifted, antique, hand-me-down, or used piece. I find this is the case with hardworking pieces like the sofa your family sits on all the time or the table and chairs that are used for daily meals. These are pieces that need to be sturdy and in good condition and that serve a specific function that might be hard to locate secondhand.

Just because a piece is new doesn't mean you can't customize it to make it your own. I do think there is hesitation to alter something when it's brand-new, out of the box, but it's easier when a piece is already wearing some signs of use and age. I would argue that customizing a new, store-bought piece is even more important when it comes to making your home unique. These are the pieces that can look trendy, common, or predictable. Customizing them is often simple and turns a mass-produced item into a one-of-a-kind find.

- **REPLACING HARDWARE:** This is the most obvious way to customize a cabinet, dresser, desk, or buffet. Knobs that come on store-bought furniture are usually neutral and cheap! Make a statement by adding some antique knobs or ones that show an intentional design choice.

- **MAKING A SLIPCOVER:** For soft furnishings, slipcovers are a great way not only to change the look of the piece but also to extend the life of the upholstery. Add a slipcover during one season, like a lightweight linen for spring and summer, and remove it for fall and winter.

- **REUPHOLSTERING:** I love the style of antique chairs, but after using many of them in my home over the years, I learned that some are just not suited for daily use. I still use antique chairs in my dining room, but I opted for new ones in the kitchen eating area. They are more comfortable, are a little larger in scale, and are certainly sturdier. I bought four chairs on sale in a neutral cream fabric, reupholstered the backs, and made a washable skirt for the seats.

- **PAINTING:** I mostly paint used pieces that are in need of refinishing, but I have painted new pieces as well. Sometimes you find the perfect piece, specifically on a deep discount, that is just the wrong color. Don't be afraid to break out the paint and make it work for your room.

The *Dos and Don'ts* of Buying Furniture

The world of furniture shopping can be over-whelming. There are just so many options! Should you buy new, used, antique, vintage, special order, ready-made? Do you buy sets? Should the pieces match? Or do you collect pieces over time? What about scale, comfort, function, style? Do you buy online, where there are more options, or in person so you can test out the piece? Where do you splurge and where do you save?

As with every other decorating decision, I want to make the blanket statement that you should go with your gut and buy the things you love. If you realize you're trying to talk yourself into liking a piece of furniture, walk away. Unless you have nowhere to sit, sleep, or eat, there isn't a reason to rush.

I gravitate toward buying used, vintage, and antique pieces. That started out of necessity, because our decorating budget was next to nothing, but it has stuck around because it plays into my high-low decorating approach, and old pieces are often built better and bring so much more character to a room. In my extensive furniture buying and selling experience, though, I've learned there are some pieces that are better to buy vintage or antique and some that are better to buy new (even used, but recently made).

OPPOSITE: Vintage French dining chairs are customized with tie-on slipcovers made out of antique grain sacks and linen.

BEST TO BUY VINTAGE OR ANTIQUE

- Occasional chairs
- Armchairs
- Dining and kitchen tables
- Side tables
- Twin and full bed frames
- Dressers
- Cabinets and cupboards
- Wardrobes and armoires

BEST TO BUY NEW (EVEN USED, BUT NEWER)

- Queen/king bed frames
- Mattresses
- Sofas and sectionals
- Shelving units to house TVs, etc.
- Desks
- Desk chairs
- Everyday kitchen chairs
- Cribs

DO: BUY PIECES IN GOOD, FUNCTIONAL CONDITION.

This may seem like a given, but when you're buying a piece that is a good bargain or the right size for a room, it can be easy to forgive major flaws that will inevitably result in regret. Take the time to make sure everything functions properly, and that the piece is usable. This is especially important when you're buying used from a scratch-and-dent sale.

A new queen-sized metal bed frame was chosen for this small guest room because of its vintage style.

DO: BUY PIECES THAT ARE A BARGAIN BECAUSE OF ISSUES THAT ARE EASY TO FIX.

There are thousands upon thousands of used or deeply discounted furniture pieces that are priced low simply because of cosmetic issues, like broken or missing hardware, scratches in the finish, or a missing nonessential piece (like a matching mirror). Look past these minor issues that are easy to fix, and snap up that bargain!

DON'T: BUY UPHOLSTERY THAT IS STINKY, SOILED, OR POTENTIALLY INFESTED.

Unfortunately, there are some beautiful pieces that are just too far gone to save. Unless you're willing to strip a piece down to the frame, stay away from any upholstery that is stinky, soiled or heavily stained, or shows signs of bugs. Always give a piece of furniture the "sniff test." Mustiness can be aired out, but strong pet or smoke odors are next to impossible to remove from all the layers of foam and batting.

DON'T: BUY PIECES THAT ARE BEYOND YOUR ABILITY TO REPAIR.

If a piece is damaged or isn't functional, don't purchase it unless you know how to fix it! Some furniture repairs are simple and straightforward, but others affect the structural integrity of the piece and are not easily fixed without some woodworking knowledge and skill. Pass up pieces if you're stumped on a solution to make it functional.

DO: BUY UPHOLSTERY COVERED IN UGLY OR DATED FABRIC, BUT OTHERWISE AWESOME!

There are some beautiful upholstered pieces that are in spectacular condition, but are wearing fabric that doesn't work with your style at all. These pieces are perfect candidates to reupholster

or update with a slipcover. In some cases, the fabric looks dated in the store but can be updated with some pretty pillows and a throw. Look for hallmarks of quality furniture like down-filled cushions, horsehair filling (as opposed to foam), and solid wood frames.

DON'T: BUY SOMETHING JUST BECAUSE IT'S CHEAP.

It is especially difficult for bargain hunters to turn down a good deal, but a piece isn't a bargain if it clutters up your home or knocks you off your decorating plan. When making a decision about buying a piece, take the price out of the equation. Would you pay full price for it? Do you have the perfect spot for it? If the answer to those questions is yes, go for it! If you wouldn't pay good money for it, it's not worth buying.

DO: BUY PIECES THAT YOU HAVE A PERFECT SPOT FOR.

When shopping for furniture, it's easy to get distracted by beautiful pieces that are not what you're looking for! Don't be swayed into buying a piece just because you love it. Make sure you have the perfect spot for a piece before bringing it home, especially if it's a larger piece! Prepare before shopping by making a list and taking measurements of the space you're hoping to fill.

If you can't tell, I could go on and on about furniture! In fact, it has been a main topic of conversation for over eleven years on my blog. If you need more information, inspiration, and instruction, you can find hundreds of posts dedicated to furniture makeovers, tutorials, upholstery, slipcovers, painting, refinishing, repair, and more on my blog, www.missmustardseed.com.

CHAPTER X

FINISHING *touches*

fin·ish	**touch**
/ˈfiniSH/	/təCH/
verb	*noun*
to bring (a task or activity) to an end; complete	a detail or feature, typically one that gives something a distinctive character

A ROOM SHOULD FEEL COLLECTED, NOT DECORATED.

—*ALBERT HADLEY*

If furniture makes the room, then accessories complete it. They are the final additions that give a room distinctive character and make it feel like yours. You see this in action when people bring reminders of home to the office or if they're in the hospital for an extended stay. A few little things can make a foreign environment feel a little bit more like home. Accessories make even more of an impact when they're the final layer of a room customized specifically for you and your family.

In a home, those finishing touches are the jewelry, the icing, the final coat of polish. They are often what differentiates a typical room from a unique and personalized room. They are the difference between a room that looks like a catalog and one that is distinct. We'll talk about some general rules and guidelines when it comes to styling, but it all boils down to intentionality, being purposeful about what we put where and why.

Knowing and Intentionally *Breaking the Rules*

I sort of hate that there even is such a thing as "decorating rules." Decorating is so personal, and it really doesn't need any guidelines or boundaries. It's not a sport or a board game. But I think the rules were developed with good intentions to help those who haven't developed their design eye. Following the rules can lead you to a well-designed room, but knowing them and intentionally breaking them can make your space (and style) unique.

THE RULE: ARRANGE ACCESSORIES IN THREES. I think this rule is a good place to start, but the rule is really about composition. It's directing people to create an arrangement that is pleasing to the eye, and for some reason, odd numbers usually look more pleasing in a vignette.

HOW TO BREAK IT: FOCUS ON COMPOSITION INSTEAD OF THE NUMBER OF OBJECTS. I typically don't pay attention to how many items I'm using, but what kind of shape the objects compose. How do the objects fill the space? Do they feel balanced? What is the shape of the space around them? It's intuitive and takes practice, but your eye will improve as you take unhurried time to experiment and figure out what you like! Sometimes one statement piece is enough. Sometimes an over-the-top arrangement of a bunch of items is just what you're going for. Experiment and take pictures of the arrangements. It's often easier to see in a photo what works and what doesn't.

THE RULE: THE FILL-IN-THE-BLANK-FRUIT-SIZE PRINCIPLE. Sometimes it's a cantaloupe or a pineapple, but the idea and spirit are the same. Don't buy any accessory for your home that's smaller than a _____. While I understand and appreciate the sentiment of this rule, which is to prevent someone from filling their home with teeny-tiny things that collectively look like clutter, I think it's a rule that has so many exceptions it might as well not be a rule. One of my very favorite things in my house is smaller than a clementine.

HOW TO BREAK IT: STYLING STRENGTH IN NUMBERS. A collection of small items will look better displayed together as one large group. All of the small pieces can then be admired as a collective whole. A great way to play with this idea is to remove all of the small items from a room and put back only the ones that can be a part of a group of same or related items. Corralling smaller items on a tray, in a large bowl or basket, or on a narrow shelf can also give them greater visual impact.

THE RULE: USE OBJECTS OF VARYING HEIGHTS. Again, this is a good place to start. Put tall pieces in the back, short ones in the front to create visual interest. But an arrangement can be just as compelling if it's very linear, like a line of bottles on a shelf.

OPPOSITE: Can you spot where styling rules are followed and broken on these built-in shelves?

HOW TO BREAK IT: REPETITION. When using a group of items together that are the same height, repetition is what makes it look striking, like a wall filled with framed botanicals that are all the same size, in the same frame, with the same mat. The lack of variation is emphasized by uniformity, making it work beautifully.

Ultimately, these are the rules I follow and would suggest to anyone asking about styling accessories and decorative items:

OPPOSITE: A row of ironstone milk pitchers along the top of the kitchen cabinets shows the power of a linear arrangement.

YOU HAVE TO LOVE IT.
**YOU HAVE TO HAVE THE PERFECT PLACE
   FOR IT.**
**YOU HAVE TO USE IT AND DISPLAY IT, NOT
   JUST OWN IT OR STORE IT.**

(I admit I sometimes break rules two and three, but I'm getting better at it!)

If all three of those boxes can be checked, then it works. Do it. Embrace it, even if it breaks a few traditional decorating rules along the way. Often, those end up being the most dynamic and interesting pieces and vignettes in a home.

Key Elements of Selecting *Custom-ized Accessories*

PERSONAL: When a piece has meaning and tells a story, it immediately feels custom and special. This is the main reason why I like using family pieces, antiques, and things I make. They all have a story, soul, and depth that new store-bought pieces just don't have. Even if I don't know the story of the piece, old pieces carry them through the scratches, initials, maker's marks, labels, and wear and tear. Each dent and ding is a part of history, and that just can't be manufactured.

UNIQUE: This is another reason why I love the sorts of pieces I just mentioned. They are unique. I get asked about the furniture and accessories often as I share my home online. Most of the time, I can't give a source. I bought it secondhand, it belonged to my Opa, I made it, I customized it. Unique objects make an uninspired home look custom.

REIMAGINED: Use new things in old ways and old things in new ways. Sometimes a new item makes sense. It's the perfect size or shape, it's practical, the color is spot-on, etc. You can make it unique by rethinking how you use it. Layer it with other pieces, pair it with an antique, use it in an unconventional way (a rug can become art, a tablecloth can be clipped up and used as a curtain panel, etc.). Antiquated pieces that are no longer functional can be used in a myriad of creative ways. A new cloche (cover) fits on an antique metal milk pail lid to make a display, a vintage locker basket keeps paper towels handy on the kitchen counter. The options really are limitless as long as you're willing to look at something with fresh eyes.

INTENTIONAL COLLECTIONS: My Oma was definitely a bowerbird, a collector of things, and that was even more evident as we were cleaning out her attic after she passed away. It was filled with collections: an enormous glass bowl of swizzle sticks, a box of campaign buttons, several five-gallon buckets filled with seashells and more containing glass telephone insulators. She loved the hunt, setting her sights on something and collecting it. I learned I acquired that trait from her, as I love combing beaches for shells and get giddy when approaching a flea market. Collecting for the sake of collecting, though, will land you with rows of five-gallon buckets filled with shells in your attic! Be intentional about your collections. As one grows, become more particular about buying pieces that are rare, unique, or fill in gaps in your collection. At some point, more just becomes more.

FOUND OBJECTS: These pieces are a double-bonus item! They are free (yay for free) and they have meaning, usually a memory attached to when and where the item was collected. I love sentimental found collections, like sands bottled up on vacation, smooth stones gathered from lakes and rivers, sea glass, feathers, pressed leaves and flowers, pinecones and seed pods. They bring a richness and texture to a home that is rare in man-made objects. My friend Cheri made a garland out of smooth stones with holes naturally worn in them that are found on the shores of Lake Michigan. They are a conversation starter and a reminder of childhood days spent at the lake.

COMPOSITION: This is the way you put things together that makes them look like "you." When someone tells me that they know a picture is mine on Instagram or Pinterest even before they see the photographer and stylist, that's one of the greatest compliments. It means I have developed a recognizable, unique style. Even if you don't share your work online, put things together the way you like them. It's okay and even better if it doesn't look like what everyone else is doing. It might be haphazard and loose, it might be tidy and symmetrical. There isn't a right or wrong, just what you like!

Project: FRAMED TEXTILES

One of the things I love about art is that it can be whatever you want it to be! You can hang just about anything on the wall. It can be crazy and huge, like a bicycle or industrial sign, or a collection of small utilitarian things like whisk brooms or antique combs. It's a way to display collections or interests, or to playfully indicate the function of the room. It's also a way to show off your heritage by displaying family pieces and to gracefully showcase found objects.

Shadow boxes are one of the many ways to display three-dimensional pieces or ones that are delicate, like antique linens and textiles. You can use shadow boxes from a craft store, make your own by extending the depth of a frame, purchase a handmade one off a site like Etsy, or use a store-bought frame that has a little bit of room between the mounting surface and the glass. For this project, I bought a couple of forty-dollar frames at a discount store that had about a ¾" space, which was enough room to mount an antique baby dress.

WHAT YOU'LL NEED

- Textile of your choice to frame
- Frame or shadow box with at least a ¼" space between the backing and frame
- Foam-core board
- Craft knife
- Measuring tape
- Ruler, yardstick, or straight edge
- Spray adhesive or hot glue gun
- Linen fabric
- Scissors
- Small stainless steel pins
- Optional materials: brown paper for backing the frame; linen hinging tape to seal backing; needle-nose pliers, hammer, and small brad nails, depending on the frame style or its construction

A FEW HELPFUL TIPS

- If the piece you want to mount in a shadow box is particularly valuable or of great importance, I would suggest leaving this project to the pros. They can make sure the piece is preserved through every step of the process using acid-free papers and glues, rust-free pins, and UV-protectant glass. It's worth the expense to preserve family history or valuable possessions.
- If you're mounting textiles, take time to wash and iron the piece. Trust me, the wrinkles and stains will drive you crazy eventually!
- Even if you're framing just a baby dress found at a yard sale, use acid-free papers and glues and stainless steel pins.
- This is a fun idea to display kids' uniforms or favorite T-shirts when they grow out of them.
- Make sure the glass is clean and you're happy with the position of the piece before you put the backing on. I'm not a perfectionist, but it's best to get this right the first time!

2.

3.

3.

4.

4.

STEPS

1. Dismantle the back of the frame by removing staples, nails, tape, paper, etc. holding the backing in place. If you are using a shadow box from the craft store, it might be as easy as opening a few clasps.

2. If the backing is rigid and will not accept pins, cut a piece of foam-core board with a craft knife to size. In the case of my project, I needed to cut the pieces to cover the entire area. Use heavy-duty spray adhesive or hot glue to affix the foam-core board to the backing.

3. Cut a piece of linen fabric in your desired color to act as a backdrop for the textile. Make sure the piece is clean and ironed. Affix it to the foam-core board with spray adhesive.

4. Position the textile onto the backing and pin it in place using stainless steel pins. Hold the piece vertically to make sure the pins are placed correctly.

5. Make sure the glass, textile, and backing are clean and free from hair, lint, dust, etc. Reassemble the frame and hang.

6. If desired, put on paper backing, sealed with acid-free linen hinging tape.

The View into
Another Room

A doorframe is not just a doorframe. It's a *frame*. Whether it's intended to or not, it frames out the view of the room that is beyond the opening and it also frames the view into the room. It could be argued that it's the largest piece of art in any particular room and being attentive to that view is an important part of decorating a space.

A couple of years into my work as a full-time blogger and freelance photographer, I started to notice this idea more. In a home with small rooms, I found it was often easier to get a wide shot of one room while standing in another. I started to love shots through doorframes that included a little peek of the room I was standing in. This simple act of looking at my home through a camera lens made me think about the views through each doorframe and be more intentional about making the view a good one.

What is the view of each room when seen from the next? How do those views lead you through your house?

When these questions are considered and taken into account during the decorating process, it forces you to be mindful of how each room relates to the others. That doesn't mean every room has to match or be painted the same color, but they converse with one another. They tell a story with a common thread that pulls one through the doorway. That common thread might be a color palette, textiles, art, or a subtle reference to the same style. It doesn't have to be an obvious connection, but one that is more intuitive. *Am*

I drawn into the room when I catch a glance of it through the doorway?

This can also help with selecting and arranging furniture. If the first thing you see when looking into a room is the back of the sofa or the broad side of an overstuffed chair, it might be worth rethinking the way the room is arranged. This shouldn't be done at the expense of the room being functional, though! *Well, the sofa no longer faces the TV, but at least it looks good from the dining room.* Let's not take it that far! But simply adding a sofa table behind the sofa or adding a little basket and a lamp next to the chair will create something that is more interesting to look at from the next room.

Styling *Secret* Weapons

Over the years, I have learned there are a few go-to things that I gravitate toward when I'm looking for accessories for styling my home, a retail space, or photos. I go to the same things for all three! They are some of the secret weapons that I use over and over again.

BOOKS

I love books to actually read (if you didn't notice from my collection of reading material), but I also use them decoratively. I particularly like old books for this purpose, but new books are on display as well. Books can be used to add color and texture to a shelf, mantel, or table, and they can also be stacked to add height to an arrangement. If something is feeling a little too short in relation to other objects in a vignette, then I reach for some books!

I buy them mostly at thrift stores, yard sales, and antique shops. I look for books with pretty spines and colors that work in my home. Old leather-bound books are particular favorites, and I try to purchase books I might reference or actually read. I typically pay between one and five dollars per book and sometimes more if they are fabulous or on a subject I love. Shakespeare and Dickens are always winners to me.

MIRRORS

I just don't know if you can go wrong with a pretty mirror. Large plate mirrors, mirrored walls and ceilings? Okay, maybe in those cases, but not with a classic mirror. They can be hung in any room in the house to add depth, to reflect light or a pretty view, and to fill up a large expanse of wall. If I'm stumped at what to hang somewhere, I'll try a mirror as a default option. Most of the time, the mirror stays.

BASKETS

I am always on the hunt for good baskets to use as pretty containers and decorative accessories. I'm not talking about the tangled mess of Easter

baskets at the thrift store and every yard sale. I'm talking about well-made, sturdy, useful baskets. I use large antique French laundry baskets and trunks on top of wardrobes and cabinets to add height and extra storage. I also use them by chairs for magazines and books. Smaller baskets are tucked into shelves to add texture, and I even use them to camouflage plastic planters. If it's a pretty basket at a good price, I'll snap it up, because I know I'll use it.

PLATES AND PLATTERS

I started decorating with plates when it was the most economical way to fill up a wall or open shelving, and I have never stopped. I still love the look of plates hung in an arrangement on a wall, stacked on a shelf, or propped up to add color and a little shine to the back of a hutch. They can also be used as trays to collect smaller items on a countertop or table or under plants to prevent water rings.

PITCHERS AND CROCKS

I have collected ironstone for almost twenty years, and pitchers, small crocks, and handle-less cups have always been my favorites. The curves, lines, and details of each one attract me for aesthetic reasons, but the pieces are also very useful. Of course, I use them for flower arrangements, but I also use them to hold paintbrushes, pens and pencils, cooking utensils, small plants, clips and erasers, and anything that will fit inside.

BOWLS

Bowls are another favorite because of their versatility. I use them to hold rolls of twine, plants, fruit, decorative items like moss balls, pinecones, seashells, a stack of tea towels, etc. They are a beautiful, simple way to group smaller items together and put them on display. Wooden dough bowls can be particularly striking.

TRAYS

I have a collection of about five or six trays that I cycle through and move around the house depending on where I want to use one. They are woven, silver, painted tole, wooden, and galvanized metal, so I have a few different options when creating a vignette. Trays act as fences around a group of items. They add another layer of color or texture, but also keep things a little neater visually. As a bonus, they can also be hung on the wall as art.

PLANTS

I know there are a lot of people with black thumbs who are going to feel immediately defensive about plants making the list. After having banished more plants to the deck to die out of my sight than I can remember, I really do get it. But live plants add so much *life* to a space!

- Think of live plants as long-term bouquets of flowers. Even with some amount of neglect, most plants are going to make it a month or two. If the plant isn't too expensive, that's a

good amount of time to enjoy it. When you view your plants this way, it's easier to enjoy them while they are alive, pitch them when they are dead, and replace them with another plant. You can even change them out seasonally.

- Pothos, also known as devil's ivy, really are the easiest to keep alive indoors. After trying many other temperamental varieties of plants, I've waved the white flag and use pothos in places I want to add a little low-maintenance live greenery.
- There is no shame in using artificial plants. I assure you that many of the plants photographed in this book didn't live in these spots for very long. They were styled, photographed, and then moved back outside or to a sunny window. Sometimes you just don't have enough light in a room or you don't want to have an entire family of plants to put on a watering schedule. There are some really lovely and realistic-looking artificial plants on the market these days. Just vacuum them every couple of weeks and give them a full bath about once a year.

These are my go-to styling pieces, but yours might be different. There really aren't right or wrong pieces to use, just the ones that speak to you.

Editing

I was introduced to this German saying last year: *Weniger aber besser*. When translated into English, it means "Less, but better." If good design could be boiled down to one all-encompassing phrase, it would be this. Less, but better. Intentional. Edited. Editing transcends styles, tastes, and aesthetics. It's universally important and always effective.

Editing isn't always removing something—let me be clear about that. Editing can be adding something, correcting something, *or* removing something. It's about making final adjustments. It's about objective, careful examinations and observations that, when explored, can make the end result better. Most rooms can be greatly improved simply by editing. What happens, though, is that we *live* in our homes. We might do some editing when we first move in or after we put a fresh coat of paint on the walls or bring in a new piece of furniture, but then we get used to things. We become blind to the decor and things that accumulate and morph over time. We stop editing.

When it comes to editing your home, a space that is ever changing and dynamic, it has to be a constant, regular process. That doesn't mean you're perpetually decorating and redoing rooms, but you're regularly assessing how the rooms have evolved. Have they stayed true to your style? Did they get knocked off course after the Christmas decorations came down or when you inherited a few pieces of furniture? Have things gotten a little cluttered over time as life happened in those rooms?

I would suggest editing your home seasonally. January when the Christmas decorations come down, spring when the weather turns nice and you can air out the house, September when school starts again, and November as you're getting ready for the holidays. Editing can be as simple as taking a picture of the space, studying it for a minute, and removing a few accessories or making some tweaks. It can be as involved as rearranging the furniture, doing a few projects, and taking every accessory out of the room to start from scratch. (I call this a room reset and I've written about it several times on my blog and in my first book, *Inspired You*.)

You can also do mini edits each time you clean. Just take a few minutes when a room is vacuumed and dusted to assess it and make some small adjustments. The point of these mini edits is not to add another to-do to your already busy schedule. Making these minor adjustments can actually help you in the long run. They can be little five-minute tasks that prevent a room from getting out of control.

The best way to do some serious editing is with a good friend or family member. They can look at your room, furniture, and accessories with a fresh lens. They will likely offer up some new ideas or possibilities and tell you when something really isn't working.

FIVE CLUES THAT A ROOM ISN'T WORKING

1. **YOU AVOID IT OR YOU'RE STALLED ON A PROJECT.** I'm talking about those rooms that have been half-finished for so long they've become a running family joke.
2. **YOU THROW MORE STUFF AT IT.** We talked about that in chapter II. It's easy to just throw more things at a space to try to fix it.
3. **THINGS CATCH YOUR ATTENTION IN A NEGATIVE WAY.**
4. **YOU KEEP ASKING FOR OPINIONS.** You know it's not working, but maybe someone will talk you into feeling like it is for a little while.
5. **YOU APOLOGIZE FOR IT.** This is a biggie and we talk more about it in chapter XI.

If a room feels off to you, try editing it first. Remove, add, correct. If it still isn't working, then start considering projects, new purchases, remodeling, etc. Always start with what's free and what you already have. It might surprise you!

Quick and Easy
Finishing Touches

While this chapter is focused primarily on the accessories, art, and decorations that make a room look personal and polished, I also want to share a few relatively quick, easy, and inexpensive customizations that can be made throughout your home:

- Paint the interior doors a color other than white (black and gray are popular choices).
- Replace cabinet and door hardware.
- Switch out a faucet.
- Replace the switch plate and outlet covers.
- Add dimmer switches or remote controls for lamps.
- Swap out a builder-grade bathroom mirror for a mirror in a pretty frame.
- Paint or swap out a vent cover or air return.
- Add chair rail.
- Change out a light fixture.

Decorate with the Mindset of a *Gardener*

If your concept of the time it takes to decorate a room comes from TV shows and social media, then I want to offer a more realistic perspective. Finishing touches take time. Sometimes everything falls into place in a few days, a few weeks, or a few months, but most of the time, beautiful rooms, character-rich, soulful spaces, take years. Years of collecting and editing. Years of experimenting and learning. Good things take time, and decorating is no different.

Sure, you can go out to the store and buy everything you need to finish a room, but making it look custom and uniquely like you isn't going to come out of a store after one shopping trip. So instead of rushing toward a finished room, decorate with the mindset of a gardener. What could things look like in one, five, or ten years? What am I planting that will be a good backdrop to flowering annuals and a framework when the leaves fall? In decorating terms, what decisions are timeless, good foundations to build around?

This is the way to create beautiful rooms. Slow down, be patient, and be persistent in the pursuit of discovering your own personal style. All of the finishing touches will spring from that.

CHAPTER XI

THE ART OF *loving*
YOUR HOME
FOR WHAT IT IS

art	**lov·ing**
/ärt/	/'ləviNG/
noun	*adjective*
a skill at doing a specified thing, typically one acquired through practice	feeling or showing love or great care

THOUGH HOME IS A NAME, A WORD, IT IS A STRONG ONE;
STRONGER THAN MAGICIAN EVER SPOKE, OR SPIRIT ANSWERED TO,
IN THE STRONGEST CONJURATION.

—*CHARLES DICKENS*

In addition to writing a blog about decorating and creativity, I also mentor creative entrepreneurs. In all of the coaching and encouraging I've done formally and informally, I've realized the most important question I can ask someone is *why*. Why do you want to start this business? Why is this important to you?

I want to pose the same question to you now. Why? Why this book? Why work on your house? I'm going to inch out on a limb here and guess that you like the idea of personalizing your house. You want it to feel more like your home. Either you're on that journey already and want some encouragement and ideas or you're figuring out where and how to start. But why? Where does that come from?

The nature of a decorating book is inherently superficial. We're talking about symmetry and color, arranging and organizing, making things pleasing visually. At first glance, it might seem petty and materialistic, and decorating can certainly end up there. But when we dig for the why, when we push into our motives, we can find something of meaning and substance. We find a desire to nest, to be creative, and to make things so they are comfortable and homey. We discover a quiet longing to leave our mark where we've been, like etching our initials into a tree.

We can also discover that we want to work on a house not because there are things we dislike about it, but because there are parts of the home that we love, even if they are small and few, and we want to love it more. And our God-given creativity spurs us on.

We can love a house both for what it is and for the potential we see in it. All of the default choices, quirky updates, and imperfections can be an invitation to something better, an invitation to change it and make it truly yours.

The Practice of
Making a Home

Making a house feel like a home is a bit of an art, which I think is why it can feel overwhelming to people who wouldn't describe themselves as being artistic or creative. It seems lofty and out of reach. But I love the definition of "art" that I selected for this chapter. It's "a skill at doing a specified thing, typically one acquired through practice." Read that carefully if you didn't catch it the first time. We're not talking about a skill bestowed on a select few at birth. The skill of making a house feel like a home comes with *practice*.

We all understand the concept of practice when we tell our kids to get out their instruments and play their scales. We understand it as we're driving them to a scrimmage to get ready for a

big game. But I don't think we often hear people talking about practicing their decorating! "Oh, I'm just going to go push some fabric samples and paint swatches around on my dining room table for a little while. You know, just to practice!"

When I was a newlywed, I would go to this wonderful local fabric store and pick up one-dollar samples and small yardage from their remnant table for five dollars per yard. I didn't have any specific projects in mind, but I bought the fabrics that appealed to me. On quiet Saturday afternoons, I would pull those fabric bits and pieces out, unfold them, sort them, put them in piles, rearrange the piles, try a new combination… It was the adult version of rearranging the furniture in my dollhouse. I have no idea how

many hours I spent doing that. Jeff would look in on me, sprawled out on the floor, surrounded by colorful, patterned squares and ask, "What are you doing?"

"Oh, I'm just playing with my fabric."

He would squint his eyes, assessing a young wife he didn't understand, and leave the room with a shrug.

I didn't realize it at the time, but I was practicing. I was playing with ideas and experimenting with color and texture. I was hungry to learn about decorating, and this was the hands-on way I could do it.

Here are just a few ways you can practice:

- Rearrange a room. Scooting furniture is a great way to get a room (and you) out of a rut.
- Take pictures of your rooms from different angles. What do you notice in a photo that you don't in person?
- Get paint swatches from the paint store and just play with them. Put them up against anything: fabrics, furniture, clothes, books, dishes. See what combinations jump out at you. (You might find an unlikely combination you love!)
- Watch a decorating show or flip through a home magazine with the intention of finding one new idea to try in your house.
- We talked about developing a furniture plan in chapter III, and that's also a great way to play. Create a to-scale version of your room on graph paper. Then cut out pieces of paper to represent your furniture. Arrange and rearrange to test out new ideas.
- Ask a friend to come over and "play" in one of your rooms with you. The two of you might get some fresh ideas from one another.

- Go to a home store with room displays and take pictures. Ikea, Anthropologie, and Pottery Barn are a few of my favorite chains for this exercise, but I love going to antique stores and markets the most. There are so many creative and beautiful displays, and I come home flush with ideas.

An important, maybe even vital, part of practicing is to learn to tell the inner critic to leave you alone while you're practicing.

I once had the opportunity to attend a songwriting workshop at a music conference with a popular Christian artist. During the open Q&A time, someone in the audience raised their hand and asked about the creative process and how to handle negative self-talk while writing and composing. The successful songwriter shared that he just plays and sings in a room alone, a recording device running in case he trips upon something good. Then the negative voice will show up. "Oh, that's bad. What are you trying to do here? Who do you think you are?"

He made the motion as if he were swatting away a fly, deterring it from buzzing around his head. He would reply out loud, "Man, leave me alone. I'm just playing and singing here."

The artist took the pressure of writing a song off the table and silenced (or at least quieted) his critic. He writes songs when he's not *trying* to write songs. He's just playing and singing, enjoying the process, and it's okay if the outcome is just a private jam session and not a radio hit.

I don't remember anything else from that songwriting workshop, but I remember that story about enjoying the process and dealing with self-criticism. The work of the inner critic is an

easy one. It just says, "No." It points out what's stupid or wrong or bad or what other people might not like. It doesn't offer anything constructive or of value. The work your creativity is doing is the difficult task. It's inventing, presenting possibilities, exploring ideas, and taking risks. That is constructive and valuable. That is the part of us we should be listening to while we're practicing.

So if your negative voice chimes in while you're shopping for fabrics or picking out paint colors, shoo it away. You're not decorating for a magazine, for critique, or for the approval of people on the internet. You're just practicing, fiddling, noodling. If you hit on something you love and something that works really well, then that's your room. If you don't, you just have more practice under your belt and more experience to draw from as you continue to work on your home.

"Practice doesn't make perfect," as the old adage says. But practice does make better.

The Perils of *Inspiration*

In those early days of studying decorating, I turned to books and magazines. I had been interested in decorating since I was a kid furnishing my dollhouse and having a strong opinion on the color of my curtains and the bedding. I used to rearrange my room as a teenager and even spent my allowance on plants and yard sale furniture. (My parents weren't sure what to make of that!) I found an abundance of inspiration in those books and magazines and even started filling a binder with clippings of rooms I liked. It was like my own little Pinterest board before Pinterest.

In addition to inspiration, though, I unexpectedly found discouragement. I was comparing my sad, tiny apartment to carefully scouted and styled homes. I was stacking my decorating budget of tens of dollars against tens of thousands. My inspiration book morphed from collected ideas to seemingly unattainable ideas.

I know this feeling is only amplified now with social media. We are seeing beautiful rooms, filtered and fluffed, styled and staged. Yes, it can be an endless well of ideas and inspiration, but it can also ensnare you in the mire of comparison. Any

[CREATIVITY] IS NOT ABOUT
LEARNING HOW TO
CREATE SOMETHING LIKE
EVERYONE ELSE,
IT'S ABOUT LEARNING HOW TO
ACKNOWLEDGE THE TRUE
VALUE OF WHAT *YOU* DO.
—PHILIPPA STANTON,
CONSCIOUS CREATIVITY:
LOOK, CONNECT, CREATE

affect on you felt toward your house is drained dry when held against such high expectations. If you find yourself slipping down that slope, turn the scrolling into something positive.

Instead of allowing comparison to discourage you, write down the things you admire about those homes and rooms. Is it color? Is there a feeling that space evokes? Is there a specific piece you're drawn to? Allow yourself to admire and appreciate that room or home for what it is without comparing it to anything else. Now, look over that list. What can you replicate? What

might work in your space and on your budget? This is a simple exercise (inspired by a similar exercise found in *Conscious Creativity*), but it swings comparison back to inspiration. It gets the wheels turning and unearths possibility.

Don't Apologize on Behalf of *Your Home*

When we had friends and guests over to our house, they would often comment on the decor, and I would quickly jump in and tell them everything that still needed to be done. A welcoming tour would turn into me berating my home and picking apart things that weren't my taste. I wanted to share my enthusiasm and excitement over those future projects, but at the heart of me rattling off the to-dos was an apology. *I'm sorry my home doesn't live up to my expectations and that it probably won't live up to yours either.*

I wince even as I'm writing this, because all of the homes I've lived in during my adult life have been lovely and deserving of appreciation. It brings to mind the photos of early pioneers in front of their sod homes. They have chickens on their laps, the children in their Sunday best, boots polished and hair bedecked in ribbons, and freshly picked melons lined up on a rickety table. I look at those pictures from the comforts of my wood-framed, drywall-clad home and see a sad house made out of dirt, but they aren't apologizing for it. They were proud of it. Proud enough to pose for a picture, which wasn't a simple task in the 1800s.

When I apologize for my home, I am forcing others to play the comparison game right along with me. And, without realizing it, I am making commentary on their home. If my home doesn't meet my standards, would theirs? Would I judge their house as harshly as I do my own?

So, I'm speaking to myself and you can just listen in. *Don't do that. Don't apologize for your home*, which is a tremendous blessing no matter the year, decor, or architecture, no matter how many projects are on the to-do list. It's still something to appreciate and cherish and not apologize for.

Assignment:
OBSERVE APPRECIATION IN ACTION

Watch how the other people (and animals) living in your house enjoy each room. Kids and animals are especially fun to observe, because they are so carefree and accepting. I did this exercise and noticed my cats sunbathing on the wooden floor that needed to be refinished. My dog curled up on fabric intended for a future sewing project. The boys on the sectional in the basement family room, laughing and wrestling, oblivious to the fact that I haven't even painted or decorated that room yet. When you see other people enjoying your home and really take note of it, it's easier to appreciate and enjoy it yourself, despite the list of projects that haven't happened yet.

The *Perks of* Patience

As I was working on home projects to photograph for this book, I felt like I was on a roll. I was decisive and everything seemed to be coming together. Projects that had lived only in my imagination, some for three years, were being realized. But then one day, when I was innocently installing and painting the paneling that now lines my office walls, deciding on wallpaper and fabric, I was absolutely stuck. It was like I hit an invisible barrier, absorbing all of the momentum and halting my progress. I started questioning

all of my decisions and ideas. My parents were here to help, we were in full-on project mode, and I was stalled in my office for over two hours, looking at paint decks and staring at the wall, hoping for the right decision to effortlessly descend upon me.

I had to take a deep breath and a step back. I was putting immense pressure on myself to make the right decisions right now. And not just one but about five simultaneously, not knowing if I would even like the first decision that subsequent decisions would be based on. I felt like I couldn't take my time and feel it out, live with it. I needed to finish it, shoot pictures for this book, and have it all be perfect.

I was no longer enjoying the process but had become a slave to the makeover. I was so wrapped up in the result that I was paralyzed from taking any steps forward.

Now, I did have deadlines and there was a point when this room needed to be photo ready, but it wasn't that morning, sitting in my chair, discouraged with myself for not knowing what to do. It didn't need to be decided within the hour. It wasn't life or death. It was a small thing that didn't have a right or wrong answer, and I could step away, work on another project, and wait for inspiration to strike.

So I ordered paint samples and worked on another project while I mulled it over. I got out of the house and found a dresser in a local consignment shop that was exactly what I had been searching for. The next day, I knew I wanted to continue on the path for the room that I was already on. I was going to follow my gut. I had my meltdown and now I could get back to work.

What I was experiencing was decision fatigue (and probably some regular old fatigue), and it's normal when tackling a bunch of projects, rooms, or decorating ideas one after another or all at once. Or even trying to fit them in between a busy work and family schedule. You make a million decisions and then get stuck on picking out a toilet or which light-switch plates to use or the grout color. You've crossed the decision threshold and you find yourself crying over 2" versus 3" slats on the blinds you need to order.

Sometimes, you need to push through and make decisions so a project can be completed, but most of the time, those deadlines are self-imposed. I have yet to have a room force me to work on it! Just take a breath for a minute or a month until you're ready.

A house is never really finished. One day, it just feels like home and continues to evolve from there.

The Delights of *Making Do*

When I first started sharing about my home and business on my blog in 2009, I was on a tight budget, *and I mean tight*. No cable, no eating out, no vacations, no splurges or treats, no clothes shopping, and definitely no buying furniture and decorations for the house. We were on a bare-bones budget. I shared about my yard sale adventures and gluing moss to tennis balls and painting walls with three half-full cans of paint mixed together that I had on hand. I was on a tight budget, so all of my decorating ideas were, too.

As my blog and business grew and decorating my house literally became a part of my job, my decorating budget slowly grew over time. The house that you're seeing now is after working on my home professionally for over eleven years, but I remember those days of decorating on a shoestring budget and making do.

I remember that place well…wanting to change your wall color and not being able to buy even a cheap can of paint. I spent all of my birthday and Christmas money on things for the house: sofas from a thrift store, low-grade unfinished hardwood flooring for the home office, and fabric for curtains. I remember debating whether or not I could afford to buy a pair of three-dollar side tables at a yard sale.

I know what it's like to choke and then despair when someone shares an "affordable project" that isn't even in your hemisphere. I know. I haven't forgotten. So, I'm saying this having lived it…

Learning how to make do is one of the best

things you can do for your home. I firmly believe that being on a tight budget pushed me creatively in ways I never would've imagined if I could've splurged on anything I wanted. I never would've learned about all of the sturdy, well-made, solid wood furniture that can be purchased secondhand. I probably would've never bothered learning to sew to replicate the high-end pillows I admired.

Starting out on a tight budget gave me the skills I needed to make my home what it is today, and I'm thankful for it. Even though I would often look wistfully at rooms I couldn't afford, I knew I was building a toolbox of knowledge and experience and that it would be useful later on.

I know that when you're in that place where you have to make do, it can be frustrating. But so many good things can come out of that season and those experiences. I want to encourage you to approach those limitations as a challenge and a growing experience, one that will serve you and your future home.

Assignment:
THE MAKE-DO CHALLENGE

Give yourself a make-do challenge. Even if you have a nice budget for working on your home, it can be a great creative exercise to challenge yourself or set some boundaries. Here are a few ideas:

- Refresh a room without spending any money.
- Cut your decorating budget to zero for one month.
- Don't allow yourself to buy something new until you've finished the projects currently on your to-do list.

The Benefits of
Gratitude

"Your home is a gift and a blessing." Those are the words that lead off day one of the thirty-one-day challenge in the book *Love the Home You Have* by Melissa Michaels. Reading those simple words pushed me into really thinking about my attitude toward my home.

In the book, Melissa encourages readers to walk around their houses and look at each room "through the lens of gratitude." It seems like a simple exercise, but when I tried to implement it, I realized how hard it was for me to look at each room for exactly what it is, not what it will be "when I'm done."

I leaned into the exercise and walked through each room in our previous home in Pennsylvania, the little Cape Cod in a poky, two-stoplight town. Through this simple exercise that took just a few minutes, I realized how much I loved the light that came into the living room and how I enjoyed the evenings when our family of four piled on the couch to watch a movie together, among many other things. As I walked from room to room, listing the things I loved in my head, my affection for the house grew. My attitude was completely different when I looked at my home through the lens of gratitude.

I also learned that I'm not one to point out flaws in things, but I am one to point out potential in everything. There's a hopefulness in seeing potential, but there is also a danger. It's easy to forget to be grateful for things as they are right now. It's easy to miss the beauty in all of the imperfections and things that are undone.

Keep that in mind as you're reading this book. I hope you're inspired to work on your house, to customize it and make it feel like a home that is uniquely yours. I hope you fill a notebook with ideas and tackle some projects. But I hope you don't lose sight of the blessing and gift it is to have a home, to have *your home*.

I hope you'll love your home for all of the wonderful things that it already is.

THE *befores*

This book features the "afters," or how a room looks right now, but all of the rooms and homes featured in this book went through a transformation. I felt it was important to show how some of these rooms started before they were customized. I hope you can see some of your own "befores" in these spaces and find inspiration and possibility for your own home.

Parsonses' foyer before; after on page 20.

Parsonses' dining room before; after on page 115.

Parsonses' kitchen before; after on page 250.

Parsonses' living room before; after on page 62.

Marian's studio before; after on page 169.

Parsonses' laundry room before; after on page 208.

Parsonses' butler's pantry before; after on page 92.

Parsonses' master bedroom before; after on page 151.

Parsonses' guest room before; after on page 163.

Millers' living room before; after on page 65.

Marian's office before; after on page 184.

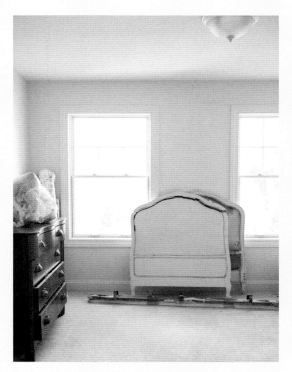

Marian's sewing room before; after on page 167.

Dietzmans' kitchen before; after on page 85.

Michael's kitchen before; after on page 101.

Millers' kitchen before; after on page 99.

Nosers' exterior before; after on page 25.

Thank you to the families who shared their homes with us:

KIRK AND CHERI DIETZMAN OF ROCHESTER, MINNESOTA

⊙ @mycottagelife

Pages 22, 40, 56 (top left), 80, 85, 102, 105, 125, 182, 195, 253 (bottom right), 264 (bottom left), 273, 281

MEGAN AND JESSE MILLER OF ALLIANCE, OHIO

⊙ @megan.d.miller

Pages 14-15, 44, 65, 99, 106 (top right), 254

Photography and styling by Megan Miller.

BRITT AND KELLY NOSER OF ROCHESTER, MINNESOTA

Pages 4, 25, 32, 38, 39, 48, 158, 198, 199, 203

KEVIN AND LAYLA PALMER OF PIKE ROAD, ALABAMA

⊙ @letteredcottage

Page 83

Photography and styling by Layla Palmer.

SHAUNNA AND ANDREW PARKER OF AUBURN, ALABAMA

⊙ @shaunnaparkerstudio

Pages 12, 304

Photography and styling by Shaunna Parker.

MICHAEL WURM JR. OF PITTSBURGH, PENNSYLVANIA

⊙ @inspiredbycharm

Pages 26, 91, 101

Photography and styling by Michael Wurm Jr.

HEATHER AND DAVE THIBODEAU OF MARYLAND

⊙ @heathered_nest

Page 159

This photo was originally published in *Cottages & Bungalows* magazine. Photography and styling by Marian Parsons, used with permission from Engaged Media, LLC.

CREDITS

acknowledgments

Thank you to my amazing family:

My husband, Jeff, for giving me (mostly) free rein to decorate this house and make it feel like ours. Thank you for all of the projects you worked on with me to bring my vision to life and for giving me all the time I needed to work on this book.

My boys, Marshall and Calvin, for being supportive of Mom's unusual job!

My parents, Warren and Kim Wagner, for traveling over one thousand miles to Minnesota to help us complete many of the projects for this book.

Thank you to my literary agent, Jenni Burke. She is one of the big reasons this book happened.

Thank you to my team at Hachette Nashville, who have been a dream to work with and consistently supportive of my vision for this book.

Thank you to all of my contributors: Shaunna Parker, Megan Miller, Layla Palmer, and Michael Wurm Jr.

Thank you to my blog readers, social media subscribers, and followers. Your support and encouragement make big dreams, like writing this book, a possibility.

FEELS LIKE HOME

sources

Many of the pieces used in my home are antiques or bought secondhand, but products and materials from these brands and stores are featured in this book. For a detailed list of product sources and paint colors, visit www.missmustardseed.com/feels-like-home-sources.

FURNITURE

Arhaus
Birch Lane
Restoration Hardware
Wayfair
Wells Works Furniture

DECOR

All-Clad
Anthropologie
Arhaus
Ballard Designs
Calphalon
Etsy
Hobby Lobby
HomeGoods
Ikea
Iris Hantverk
Jenny Steffens Hobick
Pine Cone Hill
Pottery Barn
Staub
Target
Walmart
Wayfair
World Market

FABRIC AND WALLPAPER

Arhaus
Decorators Best
Etsy
Fabrics-store.com
French General
Lisa Fine Textiles
P Kaufmann
Pindler
Pine Cone Hill
Schumacher
Select Wallpaper
STOF
Waverly

RUGS

Dash & Albert
Pottery Barn
Rugs USA
Wayfair

PAINT

Annie Sloan's Chalk Paint
Benjamin Moore
Farrow & Ball
Mango Paint
Miss Mustard Seed's Milk Paint
Sherwin Williams
Zinsser

ANTIQUES AND HANDMADE

Alice & Jay
Carried Away Antiques
Dreamy Whites Lifestyle
Dunn by Designs
eBay
Etsy
Jaysworld Books
Linen Bee
Penny & Ivy
Sylvan Clay Works

OTHER

Build.com
Delta Faucets
Hanstone Quartz
Home Depot
Kitchen Aid
LG
Marble Warehouse
Menards
Rejuvenation
Select Blinds

index

Numbers

1940s Cape Cod house, 66, 69
1950s suburban home, 26
1970s suburban home, 25

A

accessories, 248, 252–254
architectural interest, 69
acrylic paint, 223–224
affordable projects, 280
air returns, 268
antiques, 239
    baby dress, 255–257
    books, 260
    buffet, 88
    buying furniture, 240–241
    cabinets, 168
    chairs, 176
    chandelier, 153
    corbels, 88
    dressers, 153
    drying rack, 210
    in foyers, 198
    French daybed, 167
    French laundry baskets, 263
    functionality of, 176, 239
    in hallways, 194
    hand-me-downs, 239
    hardware, 176, 239
    hooks, 210
    jelly cupboards, 42–43
    Jenny Lind daybed, 153
    linens, 176
    mirror frame, 222
    in modern homes, 25
    napkins, 129
    oak hutch, 51
    painting, 234
    pine hutch, 235
    portraits, 39
    rugs, 204, 210
    shutters, 153

signs, 210
sinks, 202
stores, 51, 275
story of, 252
textiles, 49
using penetrating finishes on, 230
wooded clogs, 198
appliances, painting, 103
architectural templates, 64
art
    as focal points, 42
    for foyers, 198
    for hallways, 197
    in laundry rooms and mud
        rooms, 210
artificial plants, 265
art studios, 168–172. *See also*
    workspaces
assignments
    creating dream kitchens, 84
    creating sanctuaries, 162
    customize without sewing, 153
    dining room assessments, 113
    finding focal points, 45
    gently pushing limits, 202
    getting out of your box, 58
    identifying style, 30
    living mood boards, 53
    painting furniture, 237–238
    playing with color, 49
    rearranging rooms on paper, 64
    reliving childhood, 161
    swapping utilitarian items, 107
    timeless test, 40
    window shopping for moldings, 70
    workspace audit, 175
author. *See* Parsons, Marian
author's home, 166
    1940s Cape Cod house, 66, 69
    bathroom decorations, 104
    carpeted staircase, 194–196
    disappointment in, 27–29

faux wood paneling in, 181
foyer of, 194
guest room, 156
home office, 166, 172
ironstone collection, 117–118
kids' bedrooms, 158–162
laundry room, 70, 209–211
learning to appreciate, 29
living spaces, 81
making feel like home, 30
master bedroom, 135–136, 150–153
mudroom, 209–211
office furniture, 176–177
painted laminate cabinets, 100
personality of, 25–27
before pictures of, 284–287
reassessing workspaces, 181
removing items in, 66, 69
replacing items, 104, 106
sewing room, 166–167, 175
silverware, 114, 117
storage pieces in bedroom, 139
studio, 168, 172
suburban home, 21
suburban kitchen, 87–88
on suite bathroom, 205–206
three-season porch, 166, 168–172
toaster oven, place for, 104
use of dining rooms, 109–110,
    114, 117–118
workspace, 165, 168–175, 183–184

B

baby dress, 255–257
bargain furniture, 243
baskets, 260–263
    bike basket, 104
    French laundry basket, 263
    locker basket, 252
bathrooms, 201–206
    colors for, 202
    decorations for, 104

bathrooms *(continued)*
   half, 201–203
   mirrors changing in, 268
   moldings for, 202
   mood boards for, 202
   renovating, 205–206
   sinks for, 202
   on suite, 205–206
   wallpaper, 202
beadboard, 70, 209
beams, box, 74–79
bedding, 139. *See also* textiles
bedrooms, 135–163
   boxy suburban bedrooms, 136–142
   customizing without sewing, 153
   decorating big rooms, 154
   decorating small rooms, 155
   for guests, 156–158
   for kids, 158–162
   making a sanctuary, 162
   making big bedrooms comfy, 150–153
   making sanctuaries, 162
   prioritizing, 162
   starched fabric wall, 144–149
   wallpaper in, 144–149
beds
   in big bedrooms, 154
   buying, 241
   choosing, 139
   as focal points, 139, 153
   French daybed, 167
   in guest room, 156
   Jenny Lind daybed, 153
   during medieval times, 136
   metal framed, 242
before pictures, 284–287
big bedrooms, 150–153
bike basket, 104
Blair, Barb, 214
bold colors, 49
books, 250
bottlenecks, 180
bowls, 263
box beams, 74–80
boxy suburban bedrooms, 136–142
Brownback, Lydia, 35
brown-tinted wax, 231
budgets, 280–282

buffet, 88
buildable finishes, 230

C
cabinets
   adding corbels, 88
   adding moldings to, 89
   antique, 168
   customizing, 88–99
   laminate, 100
   in laundry rooms, 209
   painting, 90–97
   removing doors on, 88
   replacing hardware, 89
   using sprayers to paint, 98
Cape Cod house, 66, 69
carpets, 194–196
chair rails, 70–73, 153, 154, 268
chairs
   buying, 241
   French dining chairs, 240–241
   reupholstering, 239
   slipcovers for, 176
chalkboards, 222
chalk-finish paint, 224–226
chandeliers, 124, 153
character, 35–59
   adding unconventional ideas, 57–58
   finding focal points, 41–45
   finishing touches, 57
   layering colors, patterns and
      textures, 45–56
   selecting statement pieces, 36–41
Child, Julia, 83
childhood bedrooms, 161
child-sized table, 40
china patterns, 129
Churchill, Winston, 17
clogs, 198
clutter
   in bedrooms, 154, 162
   in foyers, 198
   in small bedrooms, 155
collections
   of books, 255
   displaying, 248, 255
   images of dream kitchen photos, 84
   intentional, 252

   ironstone, 209–210, 252, 263
   of old brushes, 231
   tableware, 127, 129
   of trays, 263
colors. *See also* paint
   choosing, 47, 53–54
   cool color palette, 49
   as focal points, 45
   for foyers, 194, 198–199
   for half bathrooms, 202
   for hallways, 196
   in laundry rooms, 210
   layering to add character, 45–56
   playing with, 48–49
   selecting for cabinets, 90, 93
   warm color palette, 49
composition, 254
corbels
   adding to cabinets, 88
   in laundry rooms, 209
couches. *See* sofas
counters
   painting, 100
   space on, 104
country house style, 25
creative spaces, 172, 190–191.
      See also studios; workspaces
crocks, 263
crystal chandeliers, 124

D
Davis, Miles, 29
daybeds, 153, 167
deal-breaker lists, 18, 21
decision fatigue, 280
decorating
   bathroom, 104
   big bedrooms, 154
   with function in mind, 107
   kids' bedrooms, 161
   kitchens, 104–107
   rules for, 248–251
   shows, 275
   small bedrooms, 155
   using plates as, 263
devil's ivy, 265
Dickens, Charles, 271
Dietzman family, 182

child-sized table, 40
kitchen renovation, 103–104
dining chairs, 240–241
dining rooms, 109–133
    assessments, 113
    changing purpose of room, 109–110
    formal, making, 124
    hand-stitched linen napkins
        for, 131–133
    painted wall murals for, 119–123
    relaxed, making, 124
    table linens, 129–130
    tableware for, 127–129
    traditional style, 113–118
dinner plates, 117
dishes, 114, 127
displays, 248
do it yourself (DIY) projects, 196
doorframes, 258–259
doors, 268
    front doors, 113
    for hallways, 196–197
    removing on cabinets, 88
dressers, 139
    antique, 153
    chalk painting, 225
    vintage, 213, 217
drying rack, 210

E

editing, 265–267
encouragement, 13

F

fabric
    in bedrooms, 139
    choosing patterns, 53
    expensive, 51
    as feature wall, 139
    large-scaled patterns, 53
    mixing and matching, 53
    ordering by yard, 51
    samples, 51, 272, 275
    shopping for, 50–51
    starched fabric wall, 144–149
    texture on, 54
    using in small bedrooms, 155
    vintage, 51

web searching for, 50
faucets, 268
faux focal point, 41–42
faux wood paneling, 181
finishes, 230–233
finishing touches, 57, 268
fireplaces, 42
flatware, 114, 127
focal points
    to add character, 41–45
    finding, 45
    in studios, 168
formal dining rooms, 124
foyers, 194–196, 198–200
framed textiles, 255–257
free objects, 252
French daybed, 167
French dining chairs, 240–241
French laundry baskets, 263
French wardrobes, 139–140
front doors, 113
function
    of big bedrooms, 154
    of laundry rooms and mud
        rooms, 210
furniture, 139–140, 213–245
    antique buffet, 88
    bargain for buying, 243
    beds, 139
        in big bedrooms, 154
        buying, 241
        choosing, 139
        as focal points, 139, 153
        French daybed, 167
        in guest room, 156
        Jenny Lind daybed, 153
        during medieval time, 136
        metal framed, 242
    buying, 178, 241–245
    chairs
        antique, 176
        buying, 241
        French dining chairs, 240–241
        reupholstering, 239
        slipcovers for, 176
    cleaning when stinks, 218–220
    customizing for home office,
        176–177

dated, 38
dressers, 139, 217
    antique, 153
    chalk painting, 225
    vintage, 213, 217
as focal points, 42
for foyers, 198
French wardrobes, 139–140
functionality of, 176, 239
with function in mind, 172
in half bathrooms, 202
hand-me-downs, 239
hutches
    antique pine hutch, 235
    hardware for, 57
    oak hutch, 51
    primitive step-back hutch,
        42–43
jelly cupboards, 42–43
in laundry rooms and mud
    rooms, 210
new, 240–241
painting, 237–238, 239
preparing to paint, 216–218
rearranging, 64, 275
repairing, 243
replacing hardware on, 239
selecting statement pieces, 38
for small bedrooms, 155
sofas
    buying new, 241
    customizing, 239
    setting up, 61, 63, 258
    as statement pieces, 41
    staying neutral, 41
storage pieces, 139
tables
    buying, 241
    child-sized, 40
    in dining room, 109
    for sewing, 167
    using brown-tinted wax on, 231
    using hemp oil finish on, 231
templates, 64
timeless, 41
using leftovers, 156
using penetrating finishes on, 230
Furniture Makes the Room (Blair), 214

G

gallery walls, 42, 44
gardeners, 268
great-grandmother Rosa, 114, 117
guest bedrooms, 156–158
guitars, 184
gutting, 103–104. *See also* renovating

H

Hadley, Albert, 247
half bathrooms, 201–203
hallways, 194–197
hand-me-downs, 239
hand mirrors, 202
hand-stitched linen napkins, 131–133
hardware
    antique, 176, 239
    on new furniture, 175
    removing on furniture, 218
    replacing, 89, 239, 268
heirloom hand-stitched linen napkins,
    131–133
hemp oil finish, 217, 230, 231
Hicks, David, 61
home
    apologizing for, 278
    appreciating, 278
    being grateful for, 283
    bringing out assets of, 33
    changes that help age well, 33
    customizing, 11–12
    deal-breaker lists for buying, 18
    listening to, 21–22
    making feel like, 272–276
    personality of, 21
    style of, 25, 29–32
home office, 172
    vs. creative spaces, 172
    customizing furniture for, 176–177
    designing around different
        tasks, 172
    injecting personality into, 181
home stores, 275
hooks
    for foyers, 198
    in laundry rooms and mud
        rooms, 210
hot-cold game, 161

house hunting, 18, 21
hutches
    antique pine hutch, 235
    hardware for, 57
    oak hutch, 51
    primitive step-back hutch, 42–43
hybrid finishes, 230

I

inspiration, 13, 276–277
inspiration boards, 183. *See also*
    mood boards
instructions, 13
intentional collections, 252
ironstone
    collections, 209–210, 263
    milk pitchers, 251
    plates, 117–118
    platters, 117–118, 153

J

Jefferson, Thomas, 11–12
jelly cupboards, 42–43
Jenny Lind daybed, 153

K

kids' bedrooms, 158–162
kitchens, 83–107
    in 1950s suburban home, 26
    creating dream kitchen, 84
    customizing cabinetry, 88–99
    decorating, 104–107
    gutting, 103–104
    painting, 100–103
    suburban kitchens, 87–88

L

laminate cabinets, 100, 209
latex paint, 226–227
laundry baskets, 263
laundry rooms, 70, 208–210
layering, 54
lighting, 268
    in bedrooms, 142
    chandeliers, 124, 153
    for hallways, 197
linen napkins, 131–133
linens, 129, 176

linseed oil, 230
living mood boards, 53, 54
living spaces, 61–81
    adding architectural interest, 69
    box beams, 74–80
    moldings for, 69–70
    physical needs of, 81
    picture frame moldings, 71–73
    rearranging furniture, 64–65
    scale and proportion, 69
    seasons of life, 81
    vision of, 64–68
locker basket, 252

M

making-do, 280–282
McKeown, Greg, 162
metal bed frame, 242–243
Michaels, Melissa, 283
milk paint, 220–223
milk pitchers, 251
Miller family, 45
mirrors, 42, 260
    changing in bathrooms, 268
    frame for, 222
    hand mirrors, 202
modern house style, 25
moldings
    adding to cabinets, 89
    for big bedrooms, 154
    in half bathrooms, 202
    for hallways, 197
    for living spaces, 69–70
    picture frame moldings, 71–73
    for stairways, 201
    window shopping for, 70
mood boards, 53, 54, 202
Moore, Julianne, 221
motivation, 13
mudrooms, 208–211
murals, 119–123, 201

N

napkins
    antique, 129
    hand-stitched linen, 131–133
    vintage, 127
negative self-talk, 275–276

new furniture, 240–241
nontraditional dining rooms, 110
Noser family, 25
    antique portrait, 39
    salvaged antique sink, 203

O

oak hutch, 51
odor-blocking primers, 220
off-the-wall ideas, 57
oil paint, 227
Oliver Jeanne, 29
on suite bathroom, 205–206
orange juicer, 107
organization, 178–184
outlet covers, 268

P

painted wall murals, 115, 119–123
painting
    appliances, 103
    cabinets, 90–97
    counters, 100
    dressers with chalk-finish paints, 225
    foyers, 194
    furniture, 237–238, 239
    laminate cabinets, 100
    in laundry rooms, 210
    with milk paint, 223
    new workspace furniture, 175
    or not painting, 234
    practicing, 99
    preparing furniture to, 216–218
    small bedrooms, 155
    with sprayers, 98
    stairways, 201
    things in kitchens, 100–103
    tile, 100
    using sprayers for cabinets, 98
    wall murals, 119–123
paint
    acrylic, 223–224
    buying, 53
    chalk-finish paint, 224–226
    choosing right kind, 220–227
    customizing, 233–234
    latex, 226–227
    milk paint, 220–223

oil paint, 227
    swatches for, 275
    thinning, 98
paneling, 181, 185–189
Parker, Dorothy, 162
Parker, Shaunna, 110, 112, 113
Parsons, Marian, 237–238. See also
    author's home
    apologizing for home, 278
    buying furniture, 241
    childhood of, 17
    deal-breaker lists, 18, 21
    decision fatigue, 279–280
    decorating conversations with
        husband, 193
    do-it-yourself projects (DIY), 196
    finding disappointment in
        inspiration, 276–277
    form versus function debate, 210
    great-grandmother Rosa, 114, 117
    guitar, 184
    hiring professionals, 196
    house hunting, 18, 21
    ironstone collection, 209–210, 263
    learning to appreciate home, 283
    love of baskets, 260–263
    love of furniture, 213–214
    love of old books, 260
    making do, 280, 282
    mentoring creative entrepreneurs,
        271
    photograph tutorials and ideas, 118
    plates as decorations, 263
    playing with fabric samples,
        272, 275
    projects
        box beams, 74–79
        framed textiles, 255–257
        heirloom hand-stitched linen
            napkins, 131–133
        installing paneling, 185–189
        observe appreciation in
            action, 278
        painted wall murals, 119–123
        painting cabinetry, 90–96
        painting furniture, 237–238
        picture frame moldings, 71–73
        starched fabric wall, 144–149

pushing boundaries, 57
    at songwriting workshop, 275
    style of, 29–30
    tableware collection, 127, 129
    tight budget, 280, 282
    use of doorframes, 258
    use of trays, 263
    view on sanding, 216, 218
passages, 194–196
past successes, 183
patience, 279–280
patterns
    large-scaled, 53
    layering to add character, 45–56
penetrating finishes, 230
personal accessories, 252
personality of home, 21
physical needs, 81
picture frame moldings, 71–73
pictures, before, 284–287
pitchers, 251, 263
plants, 263–265
plates
    as decorations, 263
    dinner plates, 117
    ironstone, 117–118
    and platters, 263
playrooms, 81
polyurethane, 230
Popple, Katy, 103
porches, 182
pothos, 265
practice, 272–275
primers
    odor-blocking primers, 220
    sandpaper primers, 219
    thinning, 98
primitive step-back hutch, 42–43
professionals, hiring, 196
project management, 207
projects
    box beams, 74–79
    framed textiles, 255–257
    heirloom hand-stitched linen
        napkins, 131–133
    installing paneling, 185–189
    make-do challenge, 282
    not working, 267

projects (continued)
    observe appreciation in action, 278
    painted wall murals, 119–123
    painting cabinetry, 90–96
    picture frame moldings, 71–73
    starched fabric wall, 144–149
proportions, 69

R

railings, 201
rearranging furniture, 64
reimagined accessories, 252
relaxed dining rooms, 124
renovating
    bathrooms, 205–206
    kitchens, 103–104
    project management of, 207
repairing furniture, 218
repetition, 251
respirator masks, 98
reupholstering, 239
rooms. See also bedrooms; dining
    rooms; home office; kitchens;
    laundry rooms; living rooms;
    mudrooms; sewing rooms;
    workspaces
    photographing, 275
    planning with to-scale
        version, 275
rugs, 204, 210
runners, 201

S

samples, fabric, 51
sanctuaries, 162
sanding, 216, 218
sandpaper primers, 219
saturation levels, 49
scale
    of bedrooms, 155
    of big bedrooms, 154
    of living spaces, 69
seasons of life, 81
seating, 57, 61–63
    in big bedrooms, 154
    chairs
        buying, 241
        French dining chairs, 240–241

reupholstering, 239
slipcovers for, 176
for lifestyle, 61
in living spaces, 61–63
sofas
    buying new, 241
    customizing, 239
    setting up, 61, 63, 258
    as statement pieces, 41
    staying neutral, 41
sewing, 153
sewing rooms, 167
shadow boxes, 255
short accounts, 180
signs, 210
silverware, 114, 117
sinks
    in half bathrooms, 202
    in laundry rooms and mud
        rooms, 210
size principle, 248
slipcovers, 175, 239
smelly furniture, 218–220
sniff test, 218
social media, 276–277
sofas
    buying new, 241
    customizing, 239
    setting up, 61, 63, 258
    as statement pieces, 41
    staying neutral, 41
soft furnishings, 198
songwriting workshop, 275
spindles, 201
spot repairs, 230
sprayers, 98
spray tents, 98
stairways, 194–196, 201
stalled projects, 267
stand-alone pantries, 93
Stanton, Philippa, 277
starched fabric wall, 139–140, 144–149
statement pieces, 36–41. See also focal
    points
storage, 178
    furniture, 139
    pieces, 139
store-bought furniture, 239

studios, 168–172
styles
    defining, 29–33
    editing, 27
    of house and personal style, 32
styling, 260–265
suburban bedrooms, 136–142
sun porch, 168–172
Suzanne Tucker Interiors, 109
swatches, fabric, 51, 272, 275
switch plates, 268

T

table linens, 129–130
tables
    buying, 241
    child-sized, 40
    in dining room, 109
    for sewing, 167
    using brown-tinted wax on, 231
    using hemp oil finish on, 231
tableware, 127–129
textiles
    antique, 49
    for bedrooms, 139, 153
    framed, 255–257
textures
    on fabric, 54
    layering to add character, 45–56
three-season porch, 166, 168–172
tile, painting, 100
timeless pieces, 41
timeless test, 40, 42
toaster oven, 104
to-scale version, 275
traditional dining rooms, 113–113
traditional house style, 25
trays, 263
trim. See moldings
trunks, 263
tung oil, 230

U

unconventional ideas
    to add character, 57–58
    adding, 58
    for new workspace furniture,
        175, 178

unique accessories, 252
upholstery, 243–244
utilitarian items, 104, 107

V

varnish, 230
vent covers, 268
vintage items
    bike basket, 104
    buying furniture, 240–241
    chalkboards, 222
    chalk painting dressers, 225
    crystal chandeliers, 124
    dressers, 213, 217
    fabric, 51
    French dining chairs, 241
    hand mirrors, 202
    hooks, 210
    locker basket, 252
    milk painting furniture, 223
    napkins, 127, 129
    orange juicer, 107
    rugs, 210
    styles, 242

vision, 64–68

W

wall murals, 119–123
wallpaper
    vs. fabric walls, 144–149
    for foyers, 198–199
    for half bathrooms, 202
    for hallways, 197
walls, bedroom, 142
wardrobes, 139
warm color palette, 49
water-based poly, 230
waterborne enamel, 227–229
waxes, 230, 231
web searching, 50
Widener, Billy, 193
Wildsmith, John, 135
window shopping, 70
wooded clogs, 198
wood paneling, 181
woodwork, 23
workspaces, 165–191
    art studios, 168–172

    audit assignment, 175
    creating work zones, 172–175
    customizing new furniture for,
        176–177
    home office
        vs. creative spaces, 172
        customizing furniture for,
            176–177
        designing around different
            tasks, 172
        injecting personality into, 181
    installing paneling, 185–189
    organizing, 178–184
    reviewing, 181
    rooms for creative space, 190–191
    sewing rooms, 167
work zones, 172–175

Wurm, Michael, 26, 103

about the author

MARIAN PARSONS is a paint and textile enthusiast and lover of all things home. She started her business, Mustard Seed Interiors, in 2008, as a way to earn extra money for groceries and diapers. What started as a local decorative painting and mural business has grown into a popular blog, *Miss Mustard Seed*, a fine art and design business, and a podcast—*The Creative Exponent* with Shaunna Parker. In addition, Marian created and launched a paint line that is sold around the world—Miss Mustard Seed's Milk Paint. Her original products and fine art have been sold at Hobby Lobby, Creative Co-op, Decor Steals, TJ Maxx, and more. Her first book, *Inspired You*, was nominated for the ECPA Christian Book Award in the category of Best New Author. Marian currently lives in Rochester, Minnesota, with her husband and two sons.

Marian regularly contributes articles and photographs to *Cottages & Bungalows*, *Romantic Homes*, *Land-Leben*, *Traumwohnen*, and HGTV.com, and her work has been featured in *Country Living*, *In Her Studio*, *Woman's Day*, *Better Homes & Gardens*, *Romantic Homes*, *American Farmhouse Style*, *Cottages & Bungalows*, *Where Women Create*, *Fresh Style*, *Make It Over*, *Watercolor Artist*, *Mary Jane's Farm*, *French Style*, the *Washington Post*, and on Fox News, NBC, CBS, and the *Nate Berkus Show*.

Would you like to connect with Marian? You can find her on the following platforms:

Website, Blog, Online Shop: www.missmustardseed.com

Instagram: @missmustardseed

Facebook: facebook.com/MissMustardSeedBlog

YouTube: Miss Mustard Seed

Pinterest: pinterest.com/MissMustardSeed

Podcast: The Creative Exponent